Yuyachkani's Human Rights Theater

Five Plays

Yuyachkani's Human Rights Theater

Five Plays

EDITED AND TRANSLATED BY

Anne Lambright

The Modern Language Association of America

New York 2025

85 Broad Street, New York, New York 10004
www.mla.org

To order MLA publications, visit www.mla.org/books. For wholesale and international orders, see www.mla.org/bookstore-orders. The EU-based Responsible Person for MLA products is the Mare Nostrum Group, which can be reached at gpsr@mare-nostrum.co.uk or the Mare Nostrum Group BV, Mauritskade 21D, 1091 GC Amsterdam, Netherlands. For a copy of the MLA's risk assessment document, write to scholcomm@mla.org.

Cover illustration: Miguel Villafañe. Photograph of performance of *Contraelviento*, directed by Miguel Rubio Zapata, 8 Festival Internacional de Teatro, Caracas, 1990.

Cover description: The cover of this book features a black-and-white photo from a performance of the play *Against-the-Wind*. The photo shows the character Coya dressed in a typical rural Andean broad wool skirt and dark wool shawl; the figure is blurred from the motion of spinning around.

Allpa Rayku, *Goodbye Ayacucho*, and *Against-the-Wind* translated by permission of Grupo Cultural Yuyachkani. *Santiago* translated by permission of Grupo Cultural Yuyachkani and Peter Elmore. *Antígona* translated by permission of Grupo Cultural Yuyachkani and Editorial Pre-Textos.

Texts and Translations 48
ISSN 1079-2538

Library of Congress Cataloging-in-Publication Data

Names: Lambright, Anne editor translator | Grupo Cultural Yuyachkani
Title: Yuyachkani's human rights theater : five plays / edited and translated by Anne Lambright.
Other titles: Yuyachkani y el teatro de los derechos humanos. English
Description: New York : The Modern Language Association of America, 2025. | Series: Texts and translations, 1079-2538 ; 48 | Includes bibliographical references. |
Identifiers: LCCN 2025015214 (print) | LCCN 2025015215 (ebook) | ISBN 9781603297035 paperback | ISBN 9781603297042 epub
Subjects: LCSH: Human rights—Peru—Drama | Social justice—Peru—Drama | Peruvian drama—20th century—Translations into English | Peruvian drama—21st century—Translations into English | LCGFT: Drama
Classification: LCC PQ8470.H86 Y8913 2025 (print) | LCC PQ8470.H86 (ebook) | DDC 892/.64083581—dc23/eng/20250614
LC record available at https://lccn.loc.gov/2025015214
LC ebook record available at https://lccn.loc.gov/2025015215

In loving memory of Laurietz Seda,

dear friend, renowned critic, devotee of Peruvian theater

Contents

Acknowledgments

Over the years, I have received much support—direct and indirect—to complete this project. I would like to expressly thank the following institutions and individuals for assistance with this work.

The Charles A. Dana Research Professorship at Trinity College, Connecticut, and research funds from Carnegie Mellon University provided key material support for research travel, transcription services, permissions, and Quechua-language editing. I am grateful to Erin Zlockie for her work transcribing *Allpa Rayku*, *Contraelviento*, and *Antígona* from print to digital forms.

I am eternally indebted to Carlos Molina-Vital for his generous and meticulous work editing and correcting the Quechua dialogue in all its variants, as well as reviewing the Quechua to English translations. This labor often included a *yapa* ("extra bit")—additional suggestions and references that I have endeavored to recognize throughout the volume and that greatly enhanced the critical annotations. This would simply not be the same work without his thorough and keen eye.

I have been fortunate to rely on the support and enthusiasm of many friends and colleagues throughout this project. I am especially grateful to Milla Riggio and Pablo Delano, fellow friends of Yuyachkani and key cohosts of the group's multiple residencies at Trinity College. My dear friend and brilliant colleague Priscilla Meléndez has been a staunch supporter of this project from its inception, and her excitement for my work carried me through more than one moment of despair. Vicky Unruh has been a source of insight and inspiration throughout my career, and I am especially grateful to her for encouraging me to propose this project for the MLA Texts and Translations series.

I owe the staff and faculty of the Department of Languages, Cultures, and Applied Linguistics at Carnegie Mellon University much gratitude for providing the ideal intellectual home to bring this project to fruition. Most especially, I thank my friends Therese Tardio, for always asking how the writing was going and not allowing me to give up, and Kenya Dworkin, for being a fabulous accountability partner and for providing meticulous feedback on the translations.

I am also very grateful to everyone at the Modern Language Association who helped bring this project to fruition—James Hatch and Erika Suffern for their shepherding of the acquisitons, permissions, and editing processes, and, most especially, Cosette Bruhns Alonso for her exceptional copyediting.

Of course, my deepest appreciation goes to the members of Grupo Cultural Yuyachkani, for their amazing work, which has been a true joy to translate, and for their willingness to generously share their time, space, and wisdom over the twenty-five years that I have been studying their work. While I have been fortunate to get to know almost all the members—actors, artists, and staff—during this time and am certainly grateful to all, special thanks for their assistance with this particular project go to Miguel Rubio Zapata, Teresa Ralli, Augusto Casafranca, Ana Correa, Débora Correa, and Socorro Naveda.

Mom, thanks for always believing in me. Corazón, Isis, Paloma, Mobéy, Maya, Felipe, Ruben, Mailén, Solèy y Rafa, gracias por ser les mejores hijes y nietes del mundo entero.

Introduction

In June 2021, members of the Peruvian theater collective Grupo Cultural Yuyachkani gathered outside its Magdalena del Mar neighborhood complex, Casa Yuyachkani, to stage a series of dramatic performance celebrations there and across Lima. The occasion? The Yuyas, as the members are affectionately known, were celebrating the group's fiftieth anniversary, making it one of the longest continually running theater collectives in the Americas.[1] Over a period of several days, beloved characters from the group's extensive repertoire, costumed and donning traditional masks, interacted with the public, sang, played a variety of instruments, danced, and commented on the times, in typical Yuyachkani fashion. While the COVID-19 pandemic prevented the celebration they had originally envisioned, the Yuyas drew on their long experience with street and festival performance and collaborative, improvisational theater-making to mark their first half century of exploring Peru's most pressing social, cultural, and political issues through theater.

Grupo Cultural Yuyachkani began in 1971 as a collective of activist-artists determined to change Peruvian society through the power of theater. The original seven actors—Augusto Casafranca, Ana Correa, Débora Correa, Rebeca Ralli, Teresa Ralli, Miguel Rubio Zapata (who is also the group's artistic director), and Julián Vargas—formed one of the most influential theater groups of the twentieth and twenty-first centuries in Latin America. Yuyachkani has participated in countless national and international festivals, led numerous workshops at universities and cultural centers, and performed extensively throughout the world. Its unique theatrical vision, which aims to represent the heterogeneity of the Peruvian nation for a diverse range of audiences—from small Peruvian highland towns, to the capital Lima, to international stages—has earned Yuyachkani its well-deserved reputation as one of Peru's premier cultural institutions.

Important early influences included Bertolt Brecht, George Bernard Shaw, Henrik Ibsen, and Arthur Miller, among others, whom the group considered "referencias obligadas para el teatro popular contemporáneo, por su indiscutible aporte terico y dramtático" ("obligatory references for contemporary popular theater, due to their undeniable theoretical and dramatic contributions"; Rubio Zapata, *Notas* 22; my trans.). Inspired by these giants of nineteeth- and twentieth-century European and North American theater, as well as the innovative techniques and socially motivated theories of the Italian director Eugenio Barba (founder of the Danish Odin Teatret) and the German writer, filmmaker, and artist Peter Weiss, the group began its theatrical activism through a form of popular theater developing across Latin America at the time, one that meant a "renovación de la escena" ("renewal of the stage"), directed towards a public "interesado en la transformación social" ("interested in social transformation"; 21; my trans.). In this sense, Yuyachkani has been in dialogue with other well-known Latin American theatrical movements from its origin, particularly Augusto Boal's Theater of the Oppressed,[2] and with major contemporary theater collectives such as Colombia's Teatro La Candelaria, Ecuador's Malayerba, and fellow Peruvian group Cuatrotablas. Yuyachkani's ongoing cross-cultural and transnational appeal is evinced by its frequent invitations to perform, to participate in festivals, and to teach workshops across the globe (thus far in over twenty-five different countries). Furthermore, Yuyachkani's annual Laboratorio Abierto ("Open Laboratory") has become an important training ground, attracting professional and student actors from almost every country in the hemisphere.[3]

The group's name, Yuyachkani, means "I am thinking, I am remembering" in Quechua, the most spoken Indigenous language in Peru and, indeed, in the Americas. The actress Teresa Ralli recounts that the name first appeared in 1970 as the title of a mimeographed pamphlet through which the newly formed collective published and distributed copies of Peter Weiss's 1968 treatise on documentary theater. The members chose a name in Quechua because of their desire to connect with what they identified as the majority culture in Peru, the Quechua-speaking and Quechua-infused *sierra*, or Andean highlands (Ralli and Bárcenas). The name Yuyachkani was thus a nod to the importance of the region and of the Quechua language in Peru, even though the group did not yet fully grasp the complexity and heterogeneity of Andean cultures in those early years.

In general terms, Peru has historically been imagined as a geographically, ethnically, and culturally divided nation, a division that has produced the national stereotypes of the modern, Westernizing, Spanish-speaking coast, dominated by the capital city, Lima; the traditional, Indigenous-mestizo, Quechua-speaking, rural Andean highlands; and the primitive, Indigenous, wild Amazon region. Often this tripartite geographical division is reduced to a concept of "two Perus," which the Peruvian writer Mario Vargas Llosa, as but one example, has defined as "two cultures, one Western and modern, the other aboriginal and archaic" (51). This binary, or trinary, is seriously flawed, both in terms of accuracy—Peru is a vastly complex, heterogenous nation, with hundreds of distinct Indigenous groups and significant Asian- and Afro-descendent populations, for example—and in terms of its implications for political and social hierarchies. Throughout its work, Yuyachkani has aimed to represent the irreducible diversity of this multilingual, multiethnic, and pluricultural nation not only in terms of the thematic content of the group's plays, but also in its aesthetics and theatrical vision.

According to Miguel Rubio Zapata, a defining moment for the group occurred in 1973, while touring the Andean highlands with its first play *Puño de cobre* (1971; *Copper Fist*). Inspired by Boal and following contemporary theatrical aesthetics, the group presented a minimal theater in open air—the actors were dressed in jeans and T-shirts and used few props. After presenting the play in the highland mining town of Allpa Mina, Rubio recounted that a miner approached them, saying, "compañeros, muy bonita su obra, lástima que se hayan olvidado sus disfraces" ("Friends, your play was very nice; it's a pity you forgot your costumes"; *Notas* 1–2; my trans.). Rubio later recalled, "Por supuesto que nosotros no nos habíamos olvidado de nada, ésa era nuestra propuesta teatral. Mucho tiempo después comprendimos por qué los mineros pensaron aquello. Faltaba algo que iba más allá de los disfraces. . . . no estábamos tomando en cuenta las expresiones artísticas de los mineros—es más, no las conocíamos . . ." ("Of course, we hadn't forgotten anything; that was our theatrical vision. Much later we understood why the miners had thought that. Something was missing that went beyond costumes . . . we weren't taking into account the miners' own artistic expressions—in fact, we didn't know them . . . "; *Notas* 2; my trans.). With that realization, the group began researching traditional songs and dances from different regions, studying characters associated with local festivals, and learning Quechua, which is spoken by an estimated four million Peruvians.[4] Some of the festivals that have most influenced the group include the Cuzco-region festivals of the Virgin of Carmen in Paucartambo and Q'oyllur Rit'i ("Snow Star") in Ausangate, and the Festival of the Virgin of the Candelaria in Puno. Characters, costumes, masks, dances, and music from these festivals repeatedly appear in Yuyachkani's work, resulting in an especially rich mask practice, not just in its plays and street performances but also in its pedagogical and therapeutic workshops.[5]

Yuyachkani's artistic, cultural, social, and political influence in Peru, and indeed in theater and human rights circles across Latin America, is undeniable. A large part of Yuyachkani's corpus has been dedicated to human rights and social justice issues that affect the country, particularly Peru's marginalized rural Indigenous-mestizo communities and urban popular classes. The group's role in political and social commentary became particularly evident during the devastating Conflicto Interno Armado (Internal Armed Conflict) between the Maoist guerrilla movement Sendero Luminoso (Shining Path) and Peruvian military forces (1980–2000), and many of its plays and performance pieces are dedicated to human rights and memory work about this period. In recognition of these endeavors, Yuyachkani earned the Peruvian National Human Rights Award in 2000, and the actors were invited by Peru's Comisión de Verdad y Reconciliación (Truth and Reconciliation Commission; 2001–03) as principal artistic collaborators in its transitional justice efforts.[6]

Yuyachkani's plays, performances, workshops, and other interventions in the Peruvian sociocultural realm investigate broader international human rights discourse—both how it is mobilized in the Peruvian context and how it might be questioned, even challenged, from the Peruvian experience. Theorists of and from the Global South have pointed to the dangers in applications of what Steve Stern and Scott Strauss term the "convenient fiction" of "universal" human rights values (3). These scholars argue that "human rights are only imaginable with appeal to the global and the universal, but they are only concrete when they are local" (4). Likewise, Walter Mignolo argues that the "'human' in human rights is an invention of Western imperial knowledge rather than the name of an existing entity to which everyone will have access . . ." (10). While Western rights discourse posits that all humans are born equal, Mignolo highlights the reality that "they do not remain equal the rest of their lives" (9). Pointing to an imperial logic behind current international human rights law and practice, Mignolo proposes a means of opposing this reality through what he defines as a "decolonial option": a move away or "de-linking" from current human rights practice (11).

Yuyachkani's plays labor within this decolonial option by grounding the group's work in Andean-Indigenous cultural values and practices. In addition to the visual aesthetic in the *mise-en-scène*—the masks and costumes drawn from Andean popular festivals and rites—many of its plays are bilingual and incorporate Indigenous and mestizo performance and dance, as well as Andean history, myth, spiritual beliefs, social practices, and cultural values. In fact, Yuyachkani's audiences have been confronted with the increasingly challenging heterolinguism employed in its plays, from the inclusion of heterogenous theatrical languages from Europe, the Andes, Asia, and other parts of the Americas to the diverse musical, corporeal, and symbolic languages often deployed within a single scene to the multilingualism of the many diverse registers of Spanish and Quechua. The group's desire to facilitate the comprehension of non-Quechua speakers has waned over time, requiring audiences to both intuit meaning from context and dramatic cues and be comfortable with the discomfort of never fully understanding the plays or their meaning.

The fiction and anthropology of the renowned Peruvian writer José María Arguedas has been a guide in Yuyachkani's explorations of heterogeneity and the tensions inherent in Peruvian culture. Through novels such as *Yawar Fiesta* (1941), *Los ríos profundos* (1957; *Deep Rivers*), *Todas las sangres* (1964; *All the Bloods*), and the posthumous *El zorro de arriba y el zorro de abajo* (1971; *The Fox from Up Above and the Fox from Down Below*), as well as numerous ethnographic essays, Arguedas sought to create a vision of Peru and its complex heterogeneity; a nation-space marked by a diversity of cultures in constant contact, conflict, and tension.[7] Arguedas's attempts to translate Andean culture to national and international audiences—asserting Andean Indigenous and mestizo cosmologies, mythologies, symbolic systems, and social practices through his literary renderings of Peru—would provide a model for negotiating Western and Andean epistemologies in Yuyachkani's theatrical aesthetics, which draws on a cosmopolitan blend of Western, Andean, and Asian performance traditions.[8]

A deeper assessment of Yuyachkani's highly original theatrics requires interrogating the group's Andeanism by placing its corpus of over thirty plays in direct dialogue with some of the most important thinkers of race and ethnicity in Peru, such as the Marxist philosopher José Carlos Mariátegui, the anthropologist José Matos Mar, the historian Alberto Flores Galindo, and the anthropologist Rodrigo Montoya, many of whom the group directly references in essays, interviews, and the plays themselves. In Yuyachkani's works the sociocultural and political categories of race and ethnicity—in this case Andean Indigenous and mestizo identities—are fully embodied, that is, expressed through language, but also through silence, emotion, sound, dance, music, dress, interactivity, relationships, time, and space. These elements are carefully chosen from a vast archive of Andean cultural expressions in order to represent a complex and nuanced expression of *lo andino* ("the Andean") that defies easy classification within established cultural performance genres.[9]

Yuyachkani is acutely aware of the diversity not just of its subject matter—the Peruvian nation—but also of its audiences. Multilingual, pluricultural, with multiple layers of meaning and registers that are comprehensible in diverse ways and most likely never completely to each individual audience member, Yuyachkani's portrait of Peru's cultural and epistemological plurality takes place not only on the level of plot but also in the staging of the challenges and possibilities of intercultural communication. Like Arguedas, Yuyachkani sees itself as communicating on a larger plane. If indeed Yuyachkani must adopt Andean performative and aesthetic modes in order to communicate to an Andean *campesino* ("peasant") population, it also needs to find a way—for practical and political reasons—to translate the Andean aesthetic to a larger national and international audience in order to facilitate mutual understanding without reducing Andean culture to easily consumable terms.

Yuyachkani Corpus

The Yuyachkani corpus is extensive and varied, including over thirty-five plays, *pasacalles* ("musical street processions"), performance-installations, and *desmontajes* ("dismantling," a form of performance working backwards to explore the creation of a play or character), as well as numerous types of pedagogical and therapeutic courses (workshops and Laboratorios Abiertos; "Open Laboratories") for actors in training and for the public, which compose an important extension of the group's political-artistic practice. Yuyachkani's objective has been to create "una teatralidad original que no viene de Europa sino que nace aquí, entre nosotros" ("an original theatricality that does not come from Europe but rather is born here, among us"; *Notas* 221; my trans.), and in this process "el reconocimiento de nuestro lado andino ha sido fundamental" ("the recognition of our Andean side has been fundamental"; *Notas* 222; my trans.) The creation of this original, Andean-informed, theatricality has become evident in several recurring themes that can be traced across multiple works: the use of history and myth to contemplate contemporary issues and create a collective national memory; the role of the artist and of theater in dialogues on national political issues; the question of what theater is and how it might be understood outside the Western tradition; the role of the embodied subject in creating, performing, and recording history; the specificity of the female sociopolitical experience and the role of women as political actors, mediators, and repository of national memory; and, as outlined above, the complex diversity of the Peruvian nation.

At the same time, Yuyachkani's dramatic explorations of Peru have spawned a particular understanding of the actors, their work, and their relationship with the audience. As Diana Taylor notes, the term *yuyachkani* "signals embodied knowledge and memory, and blurs the line between thinking subjects and the subjects of thought. . . . 'I' and 'you' are the product of each other's experiences and memories, of historical trauma, of enacted space, of socio-political crisis" (*Archive* 191). Magaly Muguercia comments on the group's overtly political exploration of subjectivity, which, in itself, carries powerful political implications. Muguercia notes that Yuyachkani's dramatic exploration endeavors to "incluir en la estrategia de lo liberador la producción de un cuerpo-sujeto capaz de intervenir en la historia" ("include in its liberating strategy the production of a body-subject capable of intervening in history"; 48; my trans.). Indeed, Yuyachkani's creative work is not limited to its staging of Peruvian issues; rather, it is an effort to forge a dynamic, ongoing dramatic conversation among the actors and their publics, where the borders between "you" and "I" are blurred—a conversation that spurs the development of new national subjects empowered to intervene in the nation, and work collectively to create a new Peru.

One of the first plays after *Puño de cobre*, and the one that debuts the distinctive Yuyachkani style, is *Allpa Rayku* (1979; *For Our Land*). Included in this volume, it presents a dramatic representation of Indigenous land takeovers in the highland province of Andahuaylas, in response to the defective and delayed implementation of Peru's 1969 agrarian reform.[10] *Allpa Rayku* was notable at the time for its use of Quechua and Andean Spanish and for its highlighting of an Andean-Indigenous perspective cultivated through unstereotypical *campesino* characters, its voicing of an Andean sociopolitical perspective, and its incorporation of popular Andean music and dances. In creating the work, the actors used the songs, dances, characters, and masks they had gathered during their travels and also incorporated understandings, practices, and processes of dramatic performance they had observed through their collective performance endeavors in various Andean communities. These encounters prompted them to question the primacy of the written text in Western dramaturgical practice and to search for "otras formas de 'escritura' teatral" ("other forms of theatrical 'writing'"; Rubio Zapata,

Notas 6; my trans.). The play, like the majority of Yuyachkani's work, is the result of the collective input of the actors, created through improvising on a set of ideas and characters, integrally incorporating music and dance, and working through multiple iterations in conversation with their publics.[11] These open and dynamic processes have led to a distinctively Yuyachkani style of performance and theater-making. At the heart of the group's creative practice is a desire to develop a theatrical language that reflects on its country's history and current sociocultural realities.

According to Miguel Rubio Zapata, during the eight-year process of creating *Allpa Rayku* the actors learned directly from peasant leaders, particularly Lino Quintanilla, secretary general of the Federación Provincial de Campesinos (Provincial Federation of Campesinos), who taught them not only about the protests and political aspects of the takeovers but also about the Comités de Distracción, or "Entertainment Committees," formed at the sites of each takeover to lift morale using a site-specific hymn and other songs often composed collectively. Quintanilla shared many of these songs with the collective, which incorporated them into the play. According to Rubio, the group learned from Quintanilla that "el campesino en su lucha por la tierra libera sus manifestaciones creativas, renueva sus expresiones artísticas" ("in their fight for land, the peasants liberated their creative forces and renewed their artistic expressions"; *Notas* 3; my trans.). Thus, *Allpa Rayku* is an attempt to dramatize not just the political struggle but also the artistic renewal of the *campesinos*, by portraying the music and dance forms that characterized their activism. *Allpa Rayku* was further informed by political speeches (including long quotations from a speech by Quintanilla), other popular songs from the Andahuaylas region, and, crucially, *campesino* gatherings where the actors performed small sketches, songs, and dances that were later incorporated in the play after the actors received feedback from the *campesinos* themselves. In this manner, *Allpa Rayku*, like many subsequent plays, is developed through an "estrecha relación con el público" ("close-knit relationship with the public"; *Notas* 5; my trans.). With this material, gathered over years and in various contexts, the actors began to improvise, aiming to "romper nuestro esquema de comportamiento urbano—tanto del cuerpo como de las ideas y el lenguaje—para sumergirnos en el mundo andino" ("break the mold of our urban behavior—in our bodies as well as our ideas and language—, to immerse ourselves in the world of the Andes"; *Notas* 7; my trans.). The actors developed characters and scenes that they created in active dialogue with *campesinos* throughout Peru, not just Andahuaylas, elaborating dramatic works "susceptibles de ser modificadas permanentemente" ("susceptible to permanent modifications"; *Notas* 7; my trans.) and constantly informed by the particular contexts of its diverse audiences. This interactive, collective, open style of creating decenters the traditional Western dramatic text and the playwright to bring a new form of dramatic expression to the Peruvian stage.

After *Allpa Rayku*, Yuyachkani continued this collaborative work practice, which they term *creación colectiva* ("collective creation") with *Los músicos ambulantes* (1983; *The Wandering Musicians*). Inspired by the musical play *Los saltimbanquis* (1976; *The Jugglers or Acrobats*), by Luis Enriquez and Sergio Bardotti, and the fairy tale "The Town Musicians of Bremen," by the Brothers Grimm, the play brings together four animal characters—a donkey, a hen, a cat, and a dog—representing the Peruvian cultural-geographic regions of the Sierra (the Andean highlands), Chincha (a coastal region with a thriving Afro-Peruvian culture), the Amazon jungle, and the northern coast, respectively. The characters work through tensions and differences to produce a collective musical performance that models national unity and harmony. As Yuyachkani describes it, "hablar de *Los músicos ambulantes* es hablar de nuestra amplia diversidad como país, de la tolerancia a nuestras diferencias, de inclusión, de integración, pero también nos lleva a reflexionar que no solo es importante hacer este reconocimiento sino empezar a trabajar en la construcción de un espíritu en común" ("to speak of *Los músicos ambulantes* is to speak of our broad diversity as a country, of tolerance of our differences, of inclusion, of integration, but it also leads us to understand that this recognition is not enough, but rather that it is important to begin to work on building a common spirit"; Grupo Cultural Yuyachkani, "Los músicos ambulantes"; my trans.). Drawing on popular mask, dance, and music traditions, *Los músicos ambulantes* quickly became one of the most beloved Yuyachkani plays, and the group still regularly performs it today.

Yuyachkani's first major collaboration with an outside author was *Encuentro de zorros* (1985; *Encounter of the Foxes*), which was written by Peter Elmore. It narrates the arrival of a *serrano* (an Andean highlander) escaping the violence of his home region by migrating to Lima, where he encounters other forms of violence as he attempts to integrate into urban culture. The play dramatizes internal migration in the 1980s, when thousands of *serranos* descended on Lima to escape the Internal Armed Conflict and the extreme poverty of the Andes, resulting in what the anthropologist José Matos Mar defines as a *desborde popular* ("popular overflowing") of Andean culture into the capital city, transforming it substantially (*Desborde popular*). Other works of *creación colectiva* that focus on contemporary urban society in Lima include *No me toquen ese valse* (1990; *Don't Play that Waltz for Me*), which examines the role of the artist in times of political unrest and violence through the spirits of two dead performers who return to the stage and review their lives. *Hasta cuándo corazón* (1994; *Until When, My Heart*) explores the inner lives, fears, and hopes of a group of seven urban dwellers, from different backgrounds, about to be evicted from their tenement house. *La primera cena* (1996; *The First Supper*), created by Ana Correa, Rebeca Ralli, and Lucía Lora, who studied and worked with the group in the 1990s, imagines a reunion of a group of friends who had promised each other in high school that they would welcome the new millennium with a first supper together. The work is one of several where the female Yuyachkani actors underscore women's issues.[12]

In several plays dedicated to some of Peru's greatest artists, Yuyachkani has highlighted some of its sources of inspiration. The centrality of Arguedas has already been mentioned; the writer appears unnamed in *Allpa Rayku*, where his most famous poem "Tupac Amaru kamaq taytanchisman" ("To our Creator Father Tupac Amaru") opens the play. *Encuentro de zorros* directly picks up the theme and mythological tropes of Arguedas's last novel, *El zorro de arriba y el zorro de abajo* (1971; *The Fox from Up Above and the Fox from Down Below*), by evoking the foxes, which Arguedas had adopted from the Huarochirí manuscript, moving them from Chimbote in the 1960s (the setting of the novel) to Lima in the 1980s, to comment on Peruvian society during the Shining Path era.[13] Yuyachkani's version of the foxes appears again in *Cartas de Chimbote* (2015; *Letters from Chimbote*), a documentary-style theater that draws on the novels and letters of Arguedas to explore the writer's life and vision, drawing parallels between Arguedas's creative and personal crises and Peruvian sociocultural realities of the time of the play's creation.

Similarly, Yuyachkani uses a historical Peruvian artist to examine national issues in *El último ensayo* (2008; *The Last Rehearsal*), which explores contemporary Peruvian history through the conversations of seven musicians preparing an homage to an elderly singer. Unnamed in the play, the singer is clearly a reference to Yma Súmac, a renowned Peruvian singer from the 1950s and 1960s whose singing and acting career, constructed almost entirely outside of Peru, garnered her international fame, while in Peru she was largely ignored or criticized. In the play her marginal position in national history is contrasted with that of two iconic Peruvian figures—the poet César Vallejo and the Marxist philosopher José Carlos Mariátegui, in what the critic Claudia Salazar refers to as a "ceremonia de reconocimiento, [que] convoca una reflexión sobre las posibilidades de construir creativamente la identidad peruana" ("ceremony of recognition, [that] invites reflection on the possibilities for creatively constructing Peruvian identity"; my trans.) and a "desconstrucción de una identidad *enlatada*" ("deconstruction of a *canned* national identity"; original emphasis; my trans.)

Artists are not the only real-life inspirations in Yuyachkani's corpus. Several works are examples of documentary theater, in the form of what the group calls a *conferencia escénica*, or dramatic conference panel. Examples of these types of plays include *Pedro Huilca, ¿Por qué matar a un obrero en el Perú?* (2017; *Pedro Huilca: Why Kill a Worker in Peru?*), which revives the memory of an important trade union leader who was killed extrajudicially by Peruvian military forces in 1992. *María J.* (2022) is a one-woman *conferencia escénica*, where Ana Correa explores the life of María Jesús Alvarado, a self-taught sociologist and teacher who fought for women's rights, and by extension the rights of children, workers, and Indigenous peoples, in early-twentieth-century Peru. *Des-conocido* (2023;

Un-known), developed and performed by Julián Vargas, is a one-man show exploring mental health issues and drawing from Vargas's work with patients in psychiatric hospitals. In typical Yuyachkani style, throughout their respective performances both Correa and Vargas weave deep personal connections with the historical figure's story, surveying their own development as artists and highlighting contemporary social issues.

While the broader Yuyachkani corpus explores a variety of human rights issues, many works center on those raised by the country's recent civil war. From 1980 to 2000, the Maoist insurgent organization Shining Path, the Peruvian military, and to a lesser extent the Marxist-Leninist rebel group, Movimiento Revolucionario Túpac Amaru (Tupac Amaru Revolutionary Movement), waged a horrifically violent war that was first concentrated in rural areas of the Ayacucho region of the highlands and eventually spread to the cities and the coast. A traumatic period of Peruvian history with ramifications to this day, the Internal Armed Conflict saw the death or disappearance of almost seventy thousand Peruvians, the majority of them Indigenous peoples targeted by both the rebels and the government (Comisión de la Verdad 13). Of the dead or disappeared, the vast majority were Indigenous or mestizo rural inhabitants, seventy-five percent Quechua-speaking—in a country where approximately twenty-five percent of inhabitants speak Quechua (13).

In this category of political theater are *Contraelviento* (1985; *Against-the-Wind*), *Adiós Ayacucho* (1990; *Goodbye Ayacucho*), *Antígona* (2000), and *Santiago* (2000), all included in this volume, as well as plays such as *Retorno* (1996; *Return*), *Rosa Cuchillo* (2002), and *Kay Punku* (2007; *This Door*). The first work to directly explore the period of terror was *Contraelviento*, which draws on Andean mythology and popular festival characters and employs a highly stylized, mythical register to tell the story of two sisters caught up in the conflict, then still largely localized in the rural Andes. With this play, Yuyachkani used its work to bring attention to and denounce a situation that many of those living in the capital saw as removed from themselves and from their responsibilities as citizens.

Yuyachkani quickly became a major voice in both exposing the realities of the violence sweeping the country and insisting on essential memory work once the conflict was declared officially over in 2000. Its works on this topic have earned the group well-deserved recognition as a major human rights advocate in Peru and beyond. Based on a homonymous novella by Julio Ortega, *Adiós Ayacucho* presents the issue of justice for the disappeared by following the journey of a deceased peasant leader as he travels from Ayacucho to Lima in search of his stolen remains. *Antígona*, the only Yuyachkani play with no direct references to Peruvian history or contemporary sociocultural realities, is a reinterpretation of the classic Sophocles play *Antigone* with text by the Peruvian poet José Watanabe. Set in ancient Thebes, the work has a single actress, Teresa Ralli, portray all the characters in an exploration of memory, truth, and justice.[14] Inspired by the group's interactions with Andean women survivors of *manchay tiempo* ("the time of fear"), *Antígona*, *Rosa Cuchillo* (based on the titular character of a 1996 novel by the Peruvian author Oscar Colchado Lucio), and *Kay Punku* make visible female experiences of war by focusing on women who confront power, seek justice, search for disappeared children, and survive sexual violence. Channeling another type of national subject created by the violence, *Retorno* is an improvisational conversation between two strangers who cross paths while returning to their highland homes after the war; this short but impactful play recounts the cyclical journeys undertaken by so many *serranos* during that period. The final play included in this collection, *Santiago*, cocreated with Peter Elmore, explores the long history of ethnic conflict and the legacy of conquest and colonization in the Andes, as played out in a small, nearly abandoned town in the immediate post-conflict era, and questions whether the country can find peace without addressing long-standing social injustices.

While Yuyachkani has received perhaps as many threats as commendations for its labors, the group has not wavered in its commitment to addressing human rights and social justice issues. Indeed, the violence explored in the plays of the Shining Path era emerges as part of a historical continuum of political instability in several performance-installation works, such as *Hecho en el Perú, Vitrinas para un Museo de la Memoria* (2001; *Made in Peru: Exhibits for a Memory Museum*), which combines visual and dramatic arts in a gallery walk that displays post-conflict urban realities. Created while the Peruvian Truth and Reconciliation Commission was conducting its public investigations, *Hecho en el Perú* provided a memory museum long before the official Lugar de la Memoria, la Tolerancia y la Inclusión Social (Place of Memory, Tolerance and Social Inclusion) opened in 2015.[15] *Sin título-técnica mixta* (2004; *Untitled, Mixed Techniques*) and *Discurso de promoción* (2017; *Graduation speech*) rely on similar museum-theater hybridizations. The former recreates the imagined attic of a history museum, filled with photos, books, speeches, clothes, and other objects of the Peruvian past that envelop the spectator in "un mundo pasado que quiere estar presente, que quiere recordarnos que esa realidad vivida es parte de la historia de todos" ("a past world that wants to be present, that wants to remind us that that lived reality is part of the history of us all"; Grupo Cultural Yuyachkani, "Sin título"; my trans.). *Discurso de promoción* emerged from one of the group's annual Open Laboratories and is the result of collaborations with other visual and dramatic artists. It revisits national myths, iconic episodes, and historical public figures to explore what Yuyachkani terms "el largo listado de deudas" ("a long list of debts"; "Discurso"; my trans.) incurred since Peru's independence in 1821.

Interestingly, Yuyachkani's fiftieth anniversary coincided with Peru's Bicentennial, a fact that was not lost on the Yuyas. New works from those years, which were also marked by the COVID-19 pandemic, brought Yuyachkani, younger actors, and a variety of artists from other creative disciplines together in collaborations that wove explorations of Peru's past and present with contemplations on the role of theater in private and public life as well as citations of previous plays. *Quiero creer que estoy volviendo* (2021; *I Want to Believe I Am Returning*) explores the artistic life of the actors as they negotiated making theater in pandemic conditions. With *El teatro es un sueño* (2022; *Theater is a Dream*), Yuyachkani characters from the past and present returned to the streets, joined by over a dozen non-Yuyachkani performers, to celebrate Yuyachkani's anniversary and "rend(ir) homenaje al teatro y la poesía" ("pay homage to theater and poetry"; Grupo Cultural Yuyachkani, "El teatro"; my trans.). These newer works, like those created in the group's first five decades and surely like those it will create in the future, reflect the democratic, open spirit of Yuyachkani's artistic practice and the group's commitment to continuously refining its craft in an effort to create truly Peruvian theater.

This Collection

This volume contains five plays that highlight Yuyachkani's sociopolitical concerns and artistic vision, with a particular emphasis on the place of Andean Indigenous cultures in the national discourse and on the effects of the Shining Path conflict on the Peruvian nation: *Allpa Rayku*; *Contraelviento*; *Adiós Ayacucho*; *Antígona*; and *Santiago*. The plays span an important period in the group's trajectory, during a time when it was cementing its practice and philosophy, and are key examples of the group's engagement with Andean culture (*Antígona*, despite its setting in ancient Thebes, was inspired by the violence in the Andes during the Internal Armed Conflict, and has been performed for Andean survivors of the war). These are among the most important of the plays that earned the group its international reputation as a major voice on human rights issues in Peru and as a model for how activist-artists can intervene in national dialogues on human rights and social justice. Furthermore, the chosen plays are among the most text-heavy, making them more appropriate than some of Yuyachkani's other plays for a printed volume—many essential Yuyachkani works are difficult to render in written mode because of the collaborative, improvisational, open forms; the heavy emphasis on song and dance; or the experimental staging, as described above. The plays in this collection have been widely documented, through online video versions, abundant still photos, and significant scholarship, so that interested readers may easily learn more about them and further appreciate their staging and critical reception.

With the exception of *Antígona*, the plays in this volume were created and are performed using Spanish and Quechua. While this is the first anthology of Yuyachkani plays with critical annotations for English-speaking audiences, *Adiós Ayacucho* and *Antígona* have both appeared previously in English-language editions, and over the past five decades significant criticism has been devoted to these plays.[16] Essential resources for further study include the Hemispheric Institute of Performance and Politics, which has collected materials related to plays created prior to 2010 (including videos, though poor in quality, of four of the plays in this volume; Grupo Cultural Yuyachkani, *Adiós Ayacucho* [*Hemispheric Institute*], *Antígona* [*Hemispheric Institute*], *Contraelviento* [*Hemispheric Institute*], and *Santiago* [*Hemispheric Institute*]), interviews, and other resources. The official Yuyachkani website, with an English option, was revised and updated for the fiftieth anniversary and contains a wealth of materials such as a complete repertoire list, with short summaries and photos of major works, and information on other Yuyachkani activities, such as the group's public demonstrations, workshops, and laboratories. The Grupo Cultural Yuyachkani *YouTube* channel (www.youtube.com/user/yuyachkani) and its *Facebook* page (www.facebook.com/grupoyuyachkani) contain a number of shorter videos and interviews that, while not accessible in English, provide a deeper understanding of the group's theatrics, aesthetics, and activities.

Yuyachkani Today

Grupo Cultural Yuyachkani continues its multifaceted theatrical engagement with Peru today. The actors are creating new plays and performance pieces while regularly performing old ones, in Casa Yuyachkani, on the streets of Lima, across Peru, and in international venues. Aware of its legacy and responsibility to the future of Peruvian theater as a driving force in national conversations, Yuyachkani continues to hold workshops for developing actors who come from Peru and from around the world. True to the group's pedagogical commitment, it holds workshops for children, using art, music, dance, and puppetry to teach about the richness of

Peruvian culture. With its firm belief in the transformative power of theater, Yuyachkani continues to offer therapeutic workshops, particularly for women who have experienced domestic violence and other traumas. In addition, Casa Yuyachkani is an important cultural institution that hosts Yuyachkani's seasonal repertoire, book launches, lectures, and exhibits. Most important, the group has continued its human rights activism across many venues; its 2023 "Teatro y memoria" ("Theater and Memory") cycle presented a series of four sold-out plays and related events to reflect on the twentieth anniversary of the publishing of the findings of Peru's Truth and Reconciliation Commission, and its members still take to the streets in important national protests. After decades of representing the cultural diversity of Peru theatrically, Grupo Cultural Yuyachkani shows no signs of slowing down, which is wonderful, because it certainly would be hard to imagine Peru without Yuyachkani.

Notes

1. Yuyachkani has commemorated historical milestones throughout its existence; the fiftieth anniversary was to be the largest and most elaborate celebration before the pandemic obstructed the original plans. For insight into previous celebrations, see Rubio Zapata, "40 años de Yuyachkani."

2. The "theatre of the oppressed," first developed by the Brazilian theater practitioner Augusto Boal in the 1970s, uses a variety of expressive techniques to educate and empower marginalized groups through highly interactive, community-based theatrical workshops and events. It is a pedagogical form that is still used today across the world to promote dialogue and work towards social change.

3. The pan-Latin American nature of Yuyachkani's collaborations and influence is evident from multiple vantage points, including their invitation to participate in the first meeting of the Escuela Internacional de Teatro de Latinoamérica y el Caribe (International School for Latin American and Caribbean Theater), held in Machurrucutu, Cuba, in

1989. Founded by the Argentine dramatist Osvaldo Dragún, the school was modeled on the Colombian author Gabriel García Márquez's Escuela Internacional de Cine y Televisión ("International School for Film and Television") in San Antonio de los Baños, Cuba. Dragún sought to create annual workshops in which the most important theater practitioners from Latin America came together to teach and exchange ideas. This first edition of the institute featured the Chilean actor, director, and mask artist Andrés Pérez, La Candelaria's Santiago García, Miguel Rubio Zapata and Teresa Ralli of Yuyachkani, and the Puerto Rican actors Antonio Martorell and Rosa Luisa Márquez.

4. Quechua is the most spoken Indigenous language in the Americas. A group of languages, varieties of Quechua are spoken by approximately eight to ten million people in northern Argentina, Bolivia, Ecuador, and Peru. While often associated with rural inhabitants, the number of urban and transnational Quechua speakers is large and growing, including in places such as North America and Europe. Only one of the original Yuyachkani actors, Augusto Casafranca, who was born and raised in Cuzco, was a Quechua speaker when the group began.

5. For more information on the importance of masks and mask-making for the group, see Gustavo Boada et al., "Rediscovering." Miguel Rubio Zapata has amassed perhaps the largest collection of traditional masks in Peru. In 2021, about 150 masks from his collection were displayed at the Centro Cultural Inca Garcilaso in Lima. See Rubio's description of some of the masks from the exhibit in "Máscaras Contadoras."

6. For more on Yuyachkani's human rights, memory, and transitional justice creative work and activism, see, for example, A'Ness; Lambright, *Andean Truths*; and Taylor, *Archive*.

7. See Lambright, *Creating*.

8. For more on how Arguedas worked to translate Andean culture to non-Andean audiences in his narrative fiction and ethnographic essays, see Cornejo Polar; Lambright, *Creating*; and Rama.

9. For a more extended examination of Yuyachkani's theorization of *lo andino* and particularly the role of Arguedas in the group's political-aesthetic development, see Lambright, "Yuyachkani's Andinismo."

10. Implemented during the military junta under the leadership of the General Juan Velasco Alvarado, the Agrarian Reform was a series of laws meant to redistribute rural lands from the hands of large landowners to the *campesinos*.

11. Grupo Cultural Yuyachkani has worked with outside authors or playwrights on only a handful of titles. Examples include *Encuentro de*

zorros (with text by Peter Elmore), *Adiós Ayacucho* (based on and citing some text from a novella by Julio Ortega), *Antígona* (with text by the poet José Watanabe), and *Santiago* (created in collaboration with Peter Elmore). The last three are included in this volume. These works are products of an intense collaboration between the authors and the actors.

12. As will be seen in this volume, women play central roles in works like *Allpa Rayku*, *Contraelviento*, and *Antígona*, as well as plays such as *Rosa Cuchillo*, *María J.*, and *Kay Punku*. For more on the role of women in Yuyachkani's ouevre, see Lambright, "A Nation Embodied."

13. The Huarochirí manuscript is a Quechua-language testament of ancient and colonial Andean religion compiled around 1600. Its creator is unknown, though the compilation was likely ordered by the Cuzco cleric Francisco de Ávila. Arguedas translated the original manuscript into Spanish in 1966. Despite their central role in Arguedas's final novel, the foxes of the title appear in only one brief scene in the manuscript. Beyond the use of the foxes in their plays, Yuyachkani has celebrated this cultural icon by incorporating a fox in its logo.

14. The use of classical Greek drama and mythologies as inspiration for theatrical explorations of contemporary Latin American realities is not unique to Yuyachkani. Indeed, Moira Fradinger identifies seventy-nine stage evocations of Sophocles's heroine, Antigone, that conform, in Fradinger's terms, "a vernacular corpus of American Antígonas with its own internal dynamics" (4). Yuyachkani's *Antígona* is among the most broadly known of these plays, along with Leopoldo Marechal's *Antígona Vélez* (Argentina, 1951), Luis Rafael Sánchez's *La pasión según Antígona Pérez* (*The Passion According to Antígona Pérez*, Puerto Rico, 1968), and Griselda Gambaro's *Antígona Furiosa* (Argentina, 1986).

15. The creation of the Lugar de la Memoria was a fraught political process. It remains a highly contested space, as revealed in March 2023 when Lima's far-right mayor briefly closed the museum on a bureaucratic technicality, which many believed to be politically motivated.

16. The 2008 English version of *Adiós Ayacucho* (Grupo Cultural Yuyachkani, *Adiós Ayacucho* [Taylor and Townsend]) is "adapted from Edith Grossman's translation of [Julio Ortega's] novella" (Taylor and Townsend 296). Neither the introduction nor the notes to this version reference the inclusion of Quechua dialogue or that the character of Q'olla does not appear in the novel. A bilingual version of *Antígona*, with a translation and two critical essays by Cristina Pérez Díaz, was published in 2023.

Works Cited

A'Ness, Francine. "Resisting Amnesia: Yuyachkani, Performance, and the Post-War Reconstruction of Peru." *Theater Journal*, vol. 56, 2004, pp. 395–414.

Boada, Gustavo, et al. "Rediscovering Mask Performance in Peru: Gustavo Boada, Maskmaker with Yuyachkani." *TDR: The Drama Review*, vol. 43, no. 3, 1999, pp. 169–81. *Project Muse*, muse.jhu.edu/article/32946.

Comisión de la Verdad y Reconciliación. *Informe Final*. CVR, 2003. www.cverdad.org.pe/ifinal/index.php.

Cornejo Polar, Antonio. *Los universos narrativos de José María Arguedas*. Losada, 1973.

Fradinger, Moira. *Antígonas: Writing from Latin America*. Oxford UP, 2023.

Grupo Cultural Yuyachkani. "Adiós Ayacucho." Unpublished manuscript.

———. *Adiós Ayacucho*. Directed by Miguel Rubio Zapata, 1990. *Hemispheric Institute*, hemisphericinstitute.org/en/hidvl-collections/item/75-yuyachkani-adios-ayacucho.html.

———. *Adiós Ayacucho*. Taylor and Townsend, pp. 291–300.

———. *Antígona*. Playscript by José Watanabe, directed by Miguel Rubio Zapata, 8 Jul. 2000. *Hemispheric Institute*, hemisphericinstitute.org/en/hidvl-collections/item/76-yuya-antigona.html.

———. *Contraelviento*. *Dramaturgia peruana*, edited by José Carlos Urioste and Roberto Angeles, Latinoamericana Editores, 1999, pp. 21–40.

———. *Contraelviento*. Directed by Miguel Rubio Zapata, 1996. *Hemispheric Institute*, hemisphericinstitute.org/en/hidvl-collections/item/128-yuya-contralviento.html.

———. "Discurso de promoción." *Yuyachkani*, 2017, yuyachkani.org/repertorio/discurso-de-promocion/. Accessed 3 Mar. 2025.

. "*Encuentro de zorros*: Una creación colectiva de Yuyachkani." *Conjunto*, vol. 81, 1989, pp. 29–50.

———. "Los músicos ambulantes." *Yuyachkani*, 1983, yuyachkani.org/repertorio/los-musicos-ambulantes/. Accessed 3 Mar. 2025.

———. *Santiago*. Directed by Miguel Rubio Zapata, 2001. *Hemispheric Institute*, hemisphericinstitute.org/en/hidvl-collections/item/116-yuya-santiago.html.

———. "Sin título, técnica mixta." *Yuyachkani*, 2004, yuyachkani.org/repertorio/sin-titulo-tecnica-mixta/. Accessed 3 Mar. 2025.

———. "El teatro es un sueño." *Yuyachkani*, 2022, yuyachkani.org/repertorio/el-teatro-es-un-sueno/. Accessed 3 Mar. 2025.

Grupo Cultural Yuyachkani and Peter Elmore. "Santiago." 2009. Unpublished manuscript.

Lambright, Anne. *Andean Truths: Transitional Justice, Ethnicity, and Cultural Production in Post-Shining Path Peru*. Liverpool UP, 2015.

———. *Creating the Hybrid Intellectual: Subject, Space, and the Feminine in the Narrative of José María Arguedas*. Bucknell UP, 2007.

———. "A Nation Embodied: Woman in the Work of Yuyachkani." *Letras Femeninas*, vol. 35, no. 2, winter 2009, pp. 133–52.

———. "Yuyachkani's Andinismo: Performing (towards) a Poetics of Race." *Poetics of Race in Latin America*, edited by Mabel Moraña, Anthem, 2022, pp. 169–84.

Matos Mar, José. *Desborde popular y crisis de estado: El nuevo rostro del Perú en la década de 1980*. 3rd ed., Instituto de Estudios Peruanos, 1986.

Mignolo, Walter D. "Who Speaks for the 'Human' in Human Rights?" *Human Rights in Latin American and Iberian Cultures*, edited by Ana Forncito et al. *Hispanic Issues Online*, vol. 5, no. 1, fall 2009, pp. 7–24, conservancy.umn.edu/bitstream/handle/11299/182855. PDF download.

Muguercia, Magaly. "Perú. Cuerpo y política en la dramaturgia de Yuyachkani." *Teatro Celcit*, vol. 9, nos. 11–12, 1999, pp. 48–57.

Pérez Díaz, Cristina, editor and translator. Antígona *by José Watanabe: A Bilingual Edition with Critical Essays*. Routledge, 2023.

Ralli, Teresa, and Pepe Bárcenas. "Yuyachkani: Repertorio 2015." Interview conducted by Carlos Carlín, Plus TV, 23 Sept. 2015. *YouTube*, uploaded by Wantan Night, www.youtube.com/watch?v=7JdymJfWwUs. Accessed 10 May 2016.

Rama, Ángel. *Transculturación narrativa en América Latina*. Siglo XXI, 1982.

Rubio Zapata, Miguel. "40 años de Yuyachkani." Interview conducted by Presencia Cultural. *YouTube*, uploaded by Yuyachkani, 28 Sept. 2011, www.youtube.com/watch?v=Uzu5J2pbnI4.

———. "Máscaras contadoras de historias." *El danzante enmascarado. Máscaras del Perú: Colección de Miguel Rubio, Centro Cultural el Inca*

Garcilaso, www.ccincagarcilaso.gob.pe/actividades/el-danzante-enmascarado-mascaras-del-peru/.

———. *Notas sobre el teatro.* Edited by Luis A. Ramos-García, Grupo Cultural Yuyachkani, 2001.

Salazar, Claudia, "Yuyachkani: El último ensayo." *E-misférica*, vol. 5, no. 2, winter 2008, hemisphericinstitute.org/en/emisferica-5-2-race-and-its-others/5-2-review-essays/performance-review-yuyachkani-el-ultimo-ensayo.html.

Stern, Steve J., and Scott Strauss. "Embracing Paradox: Human Rights in the Golden Age." *The Human Rights Paradox: Universality and Its Discontents*, edited by Stern and Strauss, U of Wisconsin P, 2014, pp. 3–28.

Taylor, Diana. *The Archive and the Repertoire: Performing Cultural Memory in the Americas.* Duke UP, 2003.

Taylor, Diana, and Sarah J. Townsend, editors. *Stages of Conflict: A Critical Anthology of Latin American Theater and Performance.* U of Michigan P, 2008.

Vargas Llosa, Mario. "Questions of Conquest: What Columbus Wrought, and What He Did Not." *Harper's Magazine*, Dec. 1990, pp. 45–53.

Watanabe, José. *Antígona: Versión Libre de la Tragedia de Sófocles.* Yuyachkani / Comisión de Derechos Humanos COMISEDH, 2000.

Weiss, Peter. "The Material and the Models: Notes Towards a Definition of Documentary Theatre." Translated by Heinz Bernard. *Theatre Quarterly* 1, no. 1, Jan.-Mar. 1971, pp. 41–43.

Additional Resources

English

Bernedo, Karen. "Dialoguing on Equal Terms with the Theatricalities of the World." Translated by Marianela Díaz Cardozo, 7 Nov. 2022, *La Escuela,* laescuela.art/en/campus/library/conversations/dialoguing-on-equal-terms-with-the-theatricalities-of-the-world-miguel-rubio-zapata.

Garza, Cynthia. "Colliding with Memory: Grupo Cultural Yuyachkani's *Sin Título, Técnica Mixta*." *Art from a Fractured Past: Memory and Truth Telling in Post-Shining Path Peru*, edited by Cynthia E. Milton, Duke UP, 2014, pp. 197–215.

Lerner Febres, Salomón. "Memory of Violence and Drama in Peru: The Experience of the Truth Commission and Grupo Cultural Yuyachkani—Violence and Dehuminization." *International Journal of Transitional Justice*, vol. 14, 2020, pp. 232–41. *Oxford Academic*, https://doi.org/10.1093/ijtj/ijz032.

Nigh, Katherine Jean. "Grupo Cultural Yuyachkani." *Fifty Key Figures in Latinx and Latin American Theater,* edited by Paola S. Hernández and Analola Santana, Routledge, 2022, pp. 221–25.

"Yuyachkani." *Hemispheric Institute*, 2024, hemisphericinstitute.org/en/hidvl-collections/itemlist/category/22-yuya.html.

Spanish

Alagna, Giosuè. "Liminalidad, comunidad y carnaval en *Adiós Ayacucho* de Yuyachkani." *Latin American Theater Review*, vol. 52, no. 1, Dec. 2018, pp. 5–23.

Diéguez, Ileana. "Escenarios Liminales: Donde se cruzan el arte y la vida (Yuyachkani . . . más allá del teatro)." *Teatro al Sur*, vol. 27, Nov. 2004, pp. 11–15.

Gonzales Durán, Pedro de Jesús. "Post-materialidad en los Andes: Espacios performativos andinos en Yuyachkani." *Latin American Theater Review*, vol. 55, no. 2, spring 2022, pp. 21–38. *Project Muse*, https://dx.doi.org/10.1353/ltr.2022.0001.

Grupo Cultural Yuyachkani. *Alma Viva*. Directed by Miguel Rubio Zapata, 8 Apr. 2002. *YouTube*, uploaded by Yuyachkani, 25 May 2021, www.youtube.com/watch?v=KRfyq1GvhfE&t=1s.

Guichot Muñoz, Elena. "'Esa era la idea, después, como receta, quedara esta confesión': Entrevista a Ana Correa del Grupo Cultural Yuyachkani." *Latin American Theater Review*, vol. 50, no. 2, spring 2017, pp. 179–86.

Persino, María Silvina. "Cuerpo y memoria en el Teatro de los Andes y Yuyachkani." *Gestos*, vol. 43, Apr. 2007, pp. 87–103.

Note on the Translation

The interpretive labor of translating Yuyachkani theater has developed beyond my initial, practical desire to share the work of one of Latin America's most important groups with my English-speaking students and has produced an outcome that I did not originally envision. Through translating the plays of a group I have researched for almost twenty years, I have developed an even deeper appreciation of Yuyachkani's own critical and theoretical contributions, which are doubtless among the most original interventions in transnational dialogues on human and cultural rights, social justice, interculturality, and decolonial discourses. Deeply engaged in what the Peruvian cultural theorist Aníbal Quijano identifies as "comunicación intercultural" ("intercultural communication")—"un intercambio de experiencias y de significaciones, como la base de una otra racionalidad que pueda pretender, con legitimidad, alguna universalidad" ("an interchange of experiences and meanings, as the basis of another rationality which may legitimately pretend to some universality"; "Colonialidad" 19–20; "Coloniality" 177)—Yuyachkani's aesthetic-political project involves multiple layers of translation, such that their creative work complicates any intent to render it in English. In translating Yuyachkani, I have found a valuable theory and practice of horizontal, decolonial, and solidary translation that informs not only the works themselves but also my work in translating them.

Translating any dramatic work is a challenge, given that the spatial-temporal coordinates of a theatrical work always exceed its written text, adding a particular level of difficulty to the fundamental one of rendering a world created within one linguistic-epistemological logic into another. Even considering this basic fact, translating Yuyachkani is not the same as translating playwrights such as Pedro Calderón de la Barca, Sor Juana Inés de la Cruz, Ariel Dorfman, or Griselda Gambaro, whose work has established text, a format that Yuyachkani actively works against. As Miguel Rubio Zapata notes, "(e)l teatro *no es literatura*, su fin no es la lectura de textos impresos, sino más bien la *lectura escénica*" ("Theater is *not literature*; its end is not the reading of printed texts, but rather the *staged reading*"; *Notas* 51; original emphasis; my trans.). It is my hope that these texts will be read in tandem with any existing video versions of the plays, where Yuyachkani realizes these staged readings and the full complexity and brilliance of its works can be appreciated.

Yuyachkani's creative practice involves improvisation and rejects the supremacy of the single-authored written text. For this reason, the version of the plays included in the volume, perhaps with the exception of *Antígona*, should be considered not as definitive but as one more rendering that honors the content and spirit of the works and the actors that created them. As of this publication, all the plays except *Santiago* have been published in some form previously, and those versions are the points of departure for the texts in this anthology. In keeping with Yuyachkani's collaborative style, the versions included in this volume are the result of comparisons with video recordings and discussions with the members of the group. Based on these additional data, for *Allpa Rayku, Contraelviento, Adiós Ayacucho,* and *Santiago,* I have made some corrections to the consulted scripts and added stage directions and descriptions for clarity when necessary. Furthermore, for *Allpa Rayku, Contraelviento, Adiós Ayacucho,* and *Santiago,* the linguist Carlos Molina-Vital has edited the Quechua dialogue to standardize spelling and assure fidelity to the linguistic variations of the Quechua language of the Andean regions represented in each play.

The texts included in this collection aim to provide English-speaking audiences with a glimpse into Yuyachkani's work. The five plays, a small fraction of a complete and coherent body of work, are themselves each incomplete. Paraphrasing Rubio in his discussion of the interaction with the miner in a production of *Puño de cobre* (*Copper Fist*), in which the miner expressed enthusiasm for the play but noted that the group's original costumes did not reflect his own, prompting Yuyachkani to transform their practice to draw on Andean theatrical traditions (1–2)—how are we to understand Yuyachkani without their costumes, music, and dances, without being present to feel their energy and participate in the collaborative endeavor that underpins their theater-making?

Yuyachkani's mission, to represent the heterogeneity of Peru in its theater, is a creative, dramatic exploration of lived social, cultural, and ethnic tensions of Peru. These translations aim to communicate those tensions as much as possible within the bounds of a printed volume. Recognizing the difficulties inherent in translating dramatic texts, which contain untranslatable, performative, and ephemeral (visual, aural, temporal, and corporeal) elements, I have endeavored to preserve the oral, physical, bilingual, and culturally heterogenous essence underlying the Yuyachkani plays. I do so in part through additional descriptions and explanations in footnotes. But also I have preserved the original Quechua within the English-language texts (supplying the English translations when necessary via footnotes or textual cues) and endeavored to capture the particular rhythms and cadences of Andean Spanish, so that the reader may experience the encounter of Western and Indigenous languages and cultures and the resulting strangeness, discomfort, and beauty of their contact.

For translations of both Spanish and Quechua, I have endeavored to keep close to the meaning without necessarily translating literally, while seeking to preserve the stylized, dramatic tone that marks the theatrical works. Further, I have left some Spanish honorifics—*don/doña, señor/señora*—and diminutives (adding the suffix *-ito/-ita* to nouns) because they do not have easy equivalents in English and yet are central to understanding the cultural variants and registers expressed in the original. Other strategic decisions particular to individual plays have been indicated in footnotes.

Works Cited

Quijano, Aníbal. "Colonialidad y Modernidad/Racionalidad." *Perú Indígena*, vol. 13, no. 29, 1992, pp. 11–20.

———. "Coloniality and Modernity/Rationality." Translated by Sonia Therborn. *Cultural Studies*, vol. 21, nos. 2–3, Mar.-May 2007, pp. 168–78.

Rubio Zapata, Miguel. *Notas sobre el teatro*. Edited by Luis A. Ramos-García, Grupo Cultural Yuyachkani, 2001.

Yuyachkani's Human Rights Theater

Five Plays

Allpa Rayku (1979)

Allpa Rayku, which in Quechua means "for our land," recounts a peasant takeover of a highland hacienda after the 1969 Ley de Reforma Agraria ("Agrarian Reform Law"), under the government of Juan Velasco Alvarado.[1] In preparation for the play, the group travelled to various villages in the highlands, learning dances and songs directly from local Andean groups. An important resource was Lino Quintanilla, secretary general of the Federación Provincial de Campesinos ("Provincial Federation of Campesinos").[2] Quintanilla provided essential insight into the *campesino* ("peasant") experiences of the takeover movement, and introduced the group to the Comités de Distracción, or Entertainment Committees, "creados en cada toma para elevar la moral de los campesinos y canalizar todo el caudal creativo desatado" ("created at each takeover to lift the spirits of the campesinos and channel the creative forces that had been unleashed"; Rubio Zapata 3; my trans.). Each recovered hacienda had its own hymn and other songs, many composed collectively, and Quintanilla had transcribed a significant number of them. All of the songs used in the play were compiled or composed by Quintanilla (Rubio Zapata 3).

In *Allpa Rayku*, Yuyachkani emphasizes how in Andean Indigenous culture, "(e)l trabajo colectivo, el esfuerzo común, se empleaban fructuosamente en fines sociales" ("collective work and common effort were employed fruitfully for social purposes"; Mariátegui, *Siete ensayos* 15; *Seven Interpretative*

Essays 4). However, even as the play criticizes the semifeudal economic structures that have oppressed Indigenous peoples, Yuyachkani moves beyond José Carlos Mariátegui's assessment of "su carácter de problema fundamentalmente económico" ("the basically economic character of the problem"; *Siete ensayos* 46; *Seven Interpretative Essays* 31), highlighting sociocultural facets. In creating this play, the group faced the challenge of popular stereotypes and superficial images through which popular culture portrayed Andean *campesinos* as either submissive or heroic, which Rubio describes as "extremos que se juntan en una misma visión ignorante de la profundidad del campesino" ("extremes that meet in a vision ignorant of the depth of the Andean peasant"; 6–7; my trans.). Contrary to those dominant visions of Andean peoples, *Allpa Rayku* presents *campesinos* and *campesinas* as politically astute, engaged, and forward-thinking as they take over land, mete out justice, and share the benefits of newly acquired ownership and power. Indeed, the play highlights sonic and visual symbols, songs, instruments, dances, costumes, and festival acts that elevate these features from mere folklore to political expression. These cultural products are at once transparent and opaque for non-Andean audiences. The public witnesses the resistance and follows the basic storyline of rebellion and social transformation; however, many cultural aspects of the play—from the Andahuaylas Quechua dialogues and lyrics of songs to the cultural significance of particular musical forms and dances to the social structures and norms—may not be fully understood. *Allpa Rayku* is the play that cements Yuyachkani's political-aesthetic framework for future theatrical approaches.

For many characters in *Allpa Rayku*, Yuyachkani recreates Spanish as spoken by Andean *campesinos* whose first language is Quechua. Centuries of contact between Spanish and Quechua has created Andean Spanish, characterized by a strong Quechua substrate that makes it deviate from more "standard" forms of Spanish. Among other characteristics, Andean Spanish suppresses definite and indefinite articles, includes the frequent repetition of terms for emphasis, overuses the gerund, and displays changes in syntax, particularly word order (Escobar 323). The English translation aims to capture the essence of that Spanish.

Notes

1. The takeover dramatized in *Allpa Rayku* closely follows a pattern of takeovers of the time. See, for example, the description by Xavier Albó of a 1976 land takeover in Chacán, which references the mobilization of *huayno* (a popular Andean music and dance genre) and Peruvian flags, the presence of the women's committee, and the orderly parceling out of the lands and sharing of work responsibilities.

2. *Campesinos* translates literally to "peasants," but campesino/campesina is used throughout in order to retain the cultural specificity of the term for the Andean region.

Works Cited

Albó, Xavier. "El retorno del indio." *Revista Andina*, vol. 9, no. 2, 1991, pp. 299–345.

Escobar, Anna María. "Spanish in Contact with Quechua." *The Handbook of Hispanic Sociolinguistics*, edited by Manuel Díaz-Campos, Blackwell, 2011, pp. 323–52. *Wiley Online Books*, onlinelibrary-wiley.com/doi/10.1002/9781444393446.ch16.

Mariátegui, José Carlos. *Seven Interpretive Essays on Peruvian Reality*. Translated by Marjory Urquidi, U of Texas P, 1971.

———. *Siete ensayos de interpretación de la realidad peruana*. 1928. Ediciones Era, 1979.

Rubio, Miguel Zapata. *Notas sobre el teatro*. Edited by Luis A. Ramos-García, Grupo Cultural Yuyachkani, 2001.

Character List

In order of appearance:

VARIOUS UNNAMED MALE AND FEMALE CAMPESINOS

CAMPESINO LEADER

THE GAMONAL

PASTORA, campesina

PAULINO, campesino

SEFERINO, campesino

TEODORO, campesino

GREGORIA, campesina

THE SMALL LANDOWNER

PANCHITO VEGA

GEORGINA, campesina

ONE

Prologue

To Tupac Amaru[1]

A group of male and female campesinos enters the stage, to the beat of a war song played on tarkas and tarolas.[2] *One carries the Tawantinsuyo flag.*[3]

CAMPESINO: Tupac Amaru, Amaruq churin, Apu Salqantaypa ritinmanta ruwasqa; llantuykin, Apu suyu sombran hina sonqo ruruykupi mastarikun, may pachakama.

Qanqa karuta, amaru ñawikiwan, wamancha kanchariyninwan, qawarqanki. Kaypin kasiani, yawarniykiwan kallpachasqa, mana wañusqa, qaparispa.

Tupac Amaru, son of the Serpent God, formed with the snow of Salqantay,[4] your shadow reaches the depths of the heart like the shadow of the mountain god, without end and without limits.

Your serpent-god eyes, that shine like the crystalline lens of all the eagles, could see the future, could see far. Here I am, strengthened by your blood, not dead, still shouting.[5]

They go out into the audience, forming groups, each one telling their story.

Campesinos with *tarkas* ("wooden Andean flutes") and *tarolas* ("snare drums") and the Tawantinsuyo flag. Photograph courtesy of Archivo Grupo Cultural Yuyachkani.

TWO
Towards the Land
By Way of Introduction

Saying "Taytáy, Mamáy,[6] ladies and gentlemen, come close," the campesinos form groups.

CAMPESINO (*Addressing a group of people*): It was the year 1974. For years and years all the campesinos, we were suffering under gamonales,[7] under bosses. I'm from Pariabamba hacienda, in the district of Cocharcas. There, in that hacienda, Manuel Escárcena was landowner and treated us like animals. Nothing, he respected. Women, he grabbed whenever he wanted. If husband complained, he tied him to the pole and with no clothes he whipped him till he grew tired. He made children, guaguitas,[8] carry chamber pots in hacienda house, collect garbage, if not, out to work in fields with no rest. When men asked for better conditions, jajayllas![9] He knocked them down with kicks or punches. Old Tayta Froilán from community, kicking belly he killed him. Afraid, we all watched. And we didn't even have any food. But finally we said, manam! No, no more. Little by little we organized to form Federation, and one 15 of July we came down from the hills like boulders, like landslide, like wild bulls to throw out

Gamonal. Arriving to hacienda, he could smell it, like he almost knew. Nighttime was turning to day and the stars were fading. It was cold, but we acted like we were cleaning ditch, lying, so he wouldn't know, when . . .

A campesino leader appears in center stage. He carries a waqra phuku.[10] *After discreetly looking around, he calls the other campesinos to complicity by sounding the waqra phuku in different directions. Upon hearing this, those who were recounting stories in different parts of the audience alternate to respond furtively using the tarkas, calling to each other, until they all come together in a single sound. Then, three campesinos enter the stage, and the rest hide among the audience.*

THREE
The Takeover

The two campesinos and campesina that have remained on stage get to work weeding the ditch. Meanwhile, the Gamonal appears with his rifle in hand.

Campesino leader: Good morning, boss, sir.
Gamonal: Good morning . . .
Campesina 3: Good morning, taytáy . . .
Gamonal: Morning . . .

Campesino 2: Good morning boss . . .

Gamonal: Good, my children, very good . . . I see you're weeding the ditch. You're up so early . . . good job. You've decided to work harder . . . Of course, the hacienda is going to be yours, isn't it? Aren't they saying the Agrarian Reform will give you my lands? Just keep on working, my children, keep on working.

Campesino leader: Boss, sir, now that they say the hacienda is going to be ours, why don't you give us a little room to spend the night . . .

Gamonal: A room??!! . . . Who do you think you are, cholo![11] Go to your shack like always! . . . Damn, what ambitions!

Campesino 2: Boss . . . then give us the upper room, the frost is really biting this year . . .

Campesino leader (*With the Gamonal distracted, he has been sneaking up and snatches away the Gamonal's rifle*): From this moment on the campesinos of the Pariabamba hacienda claim back our lands, which you have taken up for yourself for so many years. We'll give you fifteen minutes to leave the hacienda.

The Gamonal tries to escape. Campesino 4 appears.

Campesino 4: You go no further, you old donkey!

The Gamonal tries to escape on another way.

Campesino 5: There, you wretched old man! You think we're going to forget how you used Timoteo for target practice, and left him disabled?

The Gamonal tries to leave by another route.

Campesina 3: You won't escape, you scoundrel. You think we're going to forget how you'd steal our cows from the mountain to feed your purebred dogs?

The Gamonal tries one last time.

Campesina 6: Stop right there! Remember Josefa, how you broke your rifle on her back because she wouldn't sleep with you!

Gamonal (*Addressing Campesino 2*): Compadre, you're my friend, help me, save me from these . . . !

Campesino 2: I'm not your compadre anymore! You just made me your friend to abuse us, to exploit us! I'm not your compadre anymore!

Gamonal (*Trying to take his stick away*): Give me that!

All the campesinos surround him. The scene freezes.

CAMPESINA 6 (*Addressing the public*): So that was how we got rid of Gamonal, that's how we recovered our land! And then we were organized. We had committees: Organization Committee, Discipline Committee, even Entertainment Committee! It wasn't carnival season, but we were very happy, so it felt like it. How were we not going to dance! We had thrown out that man, and we felt happiness here inside. How could we not celebrate! So, we danced, and we sang very happily! (*She exits running.*)

The campesinos laugh and cry out joyfully.

Confronting the Gamonal at an open-air performance. Photograph courtesy of Archivo Grupo Cultural Yuyachkani.

FOUR
Carnival

Campesinos enter dancing and singing around a large puppet dressed in the Gamonal's clothes.

ALL (*singing*):

Carnavales '74
maytam, kaytam hamullarqanki
Andahualyaspi campesino
huñunchaykuq.
Chay campesino huñunchasqaykim
hatunsayaspa kallpanchakuykuspan
gamonalista campomanta
qarquykuchkan.
Huancahuachu haciendapis
Toxamallay haciendapis
chiki tuku waqaykuchkan
gamonalista wañunanta
yachaykuspa
Explotador kasqaykipis
Dominador kasqaykipis
qunqay wañuy hapillasuptiki
campanallaña dublaykuspa
waqaykuchkan.[12]

While the dancing and singing go on, different campesinos speak.

Campesino 1: In the Huancahuacho hacienda, in the Pariabamba hacienda, the evil owl is singing, foretelling your death, the bells are ringing, death has struck you because you were an exploiter.

Campesino 2 (*A little tipsy*): On July 15, we recovered our hacienda. No little policemen and no little gamonales can stop us campesinos.

Campesino 3: With our life or with our death, we campesinos will defend.

Campesina 4: For a miserable dime, for a miserable penny, these gamonales have exploited us. Where's that exploitation now? We made it disappear forever!

Campesino 2: Cañazo de Huancahuacho, relieve my anger; I'm so furious at Buleje, at Vergara.[13]

Campesino 5: Orange of Qollpakuchu, refresh my heart, for I am enraged at the Gamonal, at SINAMOS.[14]

Campesino 3: Come in, come in. I have my waraka,[15] too, I have my sword, too, even though you call me your brother, I'll toss you to the river.

A campesino shouts, and all dance, going the other way, now singing Huancahuachullay.

ALL:

Huancahuachullay haciendanchiktam (*bis*)
15 de julio kutichikurqanchik (*bis*)
Gamonalchapas, policiachapas (*bis*)
manas atinchu campesinutaqa (*bis*)
Mediochamanta, realchamanta
Gamonalkuna llamkachiwarqanchik
Maytaq kunan chay explotación
Wiñaypaqñam chinkachirqanchik.
Kawsaywanpas, wañuywanpas
Allpanchiktaqa defendesunmi
Yawarninchikta chaqchustinpas
Campesinuqa siempres luchasun
(*Fuga*)
Huancahuachullay cañazu
culerachayta curtaykuy
sinchi rabiasqam hamuni
gamonalchapa causanpi
sinamuschapa causanpi
Qullpakuchullay naranja
Sunquchallayta frescaykuy
Sinchi rabiasqam hamuni
Vergarachapa causanpi
Bulejechapa causanpi
Yaykulla, yaykuykamuyqa
Chayaylla, chayaykamuyqa

Warakachaypas kachkanmi
Espadachaypas kachkanmi
Maski kuyasqaypas kachkay
Maski wayllusqaypas kachkay
Amayá wawqi nichkaqtam
Mayuman wikchuykusqayki
Qaqaman tanqaykusqayki.[16]

All the campesinos exit dancing.

FIVE
The Production

Enter Pastora carrying small sacks; she sits in the center of the stage. Paulino and Seferino appear from behind, singing.

Pretty Andahuaylina,[17]
why do I love you so?
why do I adore you so?
When in the world, in my lands,
so many beauties there are.
Sighs to the wind, I send you,
I am sending you
since we met.
I'm wasting away,
dying out, yaw mana kuyana[18]

Oh, little cane of the sugar fields
empty little heartless cane,
if you don't love me
what am I to do?
If I go, it's all over,
it's all, all over.

Pastora: Hananáy, llikisqamá kachkasqa, Maypichá yawri kachkan . . .

Kaypiyá kachkasqa, kunanqa entonces, utqaytam llankasaq.[19]

Paulino: Pastorita, yaw, hamuyyá, uyariy, chakratam risun. Manam nipipas kanchu. Utqayta Pastora.[20]

Pastora: Yaw, pasapuy, mamitaymi hamunqa.[21]

Paulino: Manam nipipas kanchu. Sapallanchik kachkanchik.[22]

Pastora: Yaw, pasapuyyá. Tayta dirigente hamunqa. Ruwanayku kachkan, siranaymi.[23] I have to sew sacks.

Paulino: Paqarin tutallamanta hatarikusun tuta llankananchikpaq. Hamuyyá.[24]

Pastora: No, manam,[25] first we have to finish the sacks. Besides, if our leader finds us fooling around in the corn fields, what would he say?

Paulino: No one will see us. Your mother has gone, too . . . Look, I've brought some booze, upyasunchik.[26]

Pastora: Manam.

Paulino: Here's some canchita, sipascha, mikuykunchik.[27]

Pastora: Let's see.

Paulino: Hurry up.

Pastora: First we work, and then we eat.

Paulino starts to take away all of the sacks that Pastora had brought. He tries to grab her; she pulls away, and a chase ensues.

Pastora: Hey, Paulino, what's your problem? Now the land is free, it's ours, and you're thinking about other things.

Paulino: It'll just be a little while.

Pastora: I don't understand, Paulino, only we campesinos know how to impregnate the land. We need to care for everything. Even the Qollpakuchu oranges, to refresh our hearts. What are you thinking!

Paulino (*Contemplating what she has said*): But, I have come to work, too. I just wanted . . .

Pastora: Then, we'll work.

Paulino (*Searching around*): Where did our sacks go?

Pastora: Let's hurry. They're needed. Finally, first harvest is ready. It's a good one.

Paulino: Selling them ourselves, we'll have enough to build school, to buy medicine . . .

Pastora: We can build a community store.

Paulino: We'll buy zinc siding and tools . . .

From the side, another campesino, Teodoro, enters; he's very upset.

Teodoro: Masiykuna![28] The police detained our harvest at checkpoint. They say we have no permission to sell.

Paulino: What?

Pastora: Imata![29]

Teodoro: They say we can only get permit to sell at government offices. They won't let us go to market. They say all the produce belongs to Gamonal. That the lands are his. Our leader has called meeting . . . I'd better go tell the other farms! (*He runs out*).

Paulino: What the hell!

Pastora: Those are lies! Gamonal is gone! The harvest is ours.

Paulino: Manam, Pastora, the harvest is not free yet. We've gotten rid of Gamonal, but governments are all the same!

SIX
The People's Tribunal

A campesina enters running.

Gregoria: Pastora, Pastora. That girl. Where have you gonc?

Pastora: Auntie Gregoria, here I am.

Gregoria: Pastorcita, hurry up, the People's Tribunal is about to begin.

Pastora: A people's trial.

Gregoria: Arí.[30] There, we'll tell everything—justice will be served. Where will you sit?

Pastora: Over here, auntie.

Gregoria: And me, just over there. Later. You'll see . . .

Enter other campesinos; they sit in front of the audience.

Leader: Before turning to the points on the agenda, we'll call roll for the leaders of the communities: Huancahuacho! Lucrepata! Wankarama!

Campesino 1: Arí, tayta![31]

Leader: Pacucha! Ongoy! Turpo! Pampachiri!

Campesino 2: Kaypi, hatun leader![32] Here!

Leader: Kakiabamba! Cocharcas! Chinchcros! Chiqmu!

Campesino 3: Present, papáy!

Leader: Pariabamba! Sondondo! Acobamba!

Campesino 4: Allinmi![33] We're all here!

Leader: San Jerónimo! Lirkay! Uripa! Chaupiurqo!

Campesino 5: Kay ñuqanchik,[34] here we are!

Leader: Soraya! Andarapa! Wankaray! Chiara!

Campesino 6: Tukuy kaypi kachkaniku![35] We're all here . . .

Leader: We are going to hold people's tribunal. Before beginning we have an important report. They have just informed us that our first harvest after land takeovers, that we thought was freely ours, is being held in the police station. This is very important masiykuna, because we are learning that recovering our lands is like having horse but no reins. For this reason, fellow masiykuna, now more than ever we have to say that our struggle is not over. The organization committee will present report on what has happened and at next meeting we will decide the next steps in our fight.

Now, back to yesterday's business, those with pending cases who want to present claims, raise your hands. Let's see . . .

Gregoria: Hatun leader, may I have the word! I would like my case to be heard. My husband has been in jail for a year now. Imprisoned because of that Panchito Vega!

Leader (*Taking notes*): Panchito Vega . . .

Gregoria: Arí taytáy, yes.

Leader: Who knows Panchito?

Campesinos: We know him . . . everyone knows him . . .

Campesino Guard 1: I know him, tayta!

Leader: Fine. Let's see, you, Campesino Guard, you will go with a defense team and bring this Panchito Vega, now!

Campesino Guard 1 exits.

Leader: Let's continue with agenda. (*Campesino Guard 2 approaches and says something in his ear.*) Let's hear case of small landowner who has come here. All right, then.

Small landowner enters.

Small landowner: Good day, Mr. Leader. I've come to present complaint against colonos.[36]

Leader: What's your name?

Small landowner: Dionisio Gonzales. I have my small farm uphill, on slopes of Pariabamba hacienda.

Campesino: What are you complaining about then, if you have small farm?

Other campesino: Yeah, right, if you have land, what are you doing here?

Leader: Let him speak! Upallaychikyá![37] Silence!

Small landowner: I'm complaining because twenty days ago colonos invaded my land. They threw me and my family out of my house. I ask them, "Who sent you?" Provincial Campesino Federation, they say. That's why I've come to present my case here, so they give me back my land. Here are property titles that I have been paying boss for years. They're signed by Dr. Notary-Lawyer. Pay receipts from boss, as well.

Campesina: Those papers are worthless here! What are you thinking?

Other campesino: Misti[38] papers, from government! Some nerve!

Small landowner: Then . . . can't we figure something out, Mr. Leader . . . ?

CAMPESINO LEADER: Figure something out? Qanqaruna,[39] what are you thinking! Uyariy, listen, campesino not for sale!

OTHER CAMPESINO: This is campesino justice! Not misti justice! Out!

There are murmurings and loud comments. Meanwhile, the leader tries to call everyone to order.

CAMPESINO: Permission to speak, comrade leader. Rimasaqyá. Wawqikuna, parlaykusun. Imataq chayri allqu michi hinachu hapikusun manam chayqa allinchu, sumaq, sumaqllata purina. Chaytachu yachachisun wawanchikta? Manam riki upachu kanchik.[40] We have to take things slow when making decisions. We're getting desperate, and we didn't even let small landowner talk. Let's see, listen to what he's thinking. Does he think like campesino he is, and his parents surely were? Or do we have here abusive campesino, who doesn't work? We need to know what he feels. Maybe he's with gamonales, with SINAMOS, with government. We have to look at him with campesino eyes, not misti eyes. If he has lands, he has people, so we have to see if he pays fairly. Let him speak. Pay rimachun.[41]

DIVERSE CAMPESINOS: Yeah . . . let him speak . . . Rimay . . . wawqíy[42] . . .

Small landowner: Besides, I'm not against taking over gamonales' lands . . .

A campesino: You should have said so before . . .

Leader: Tell us, how many hectares do you have?

Small landowner: Four . . . and a little more . . .

Leader: And how many workers?

Small landowner: Two workers. We work together, them and my family. I pay them well. They're happy.

A campesino: You work? Let's see, qawachiy makiykita.[43] Show me your hands!

Small landowner (*Showing his hands*): So, here they are. Don't you know hands of a worker? I've worked my whole life!

Another campesino: Hatun leader! Permission to speak! I know Dionisio Gonzales's workers! They're my relatives. He tells truth.

General comments: Must be, then . . . How could it be? . . . What's going on? . . .

Leader: Enough. We'll make a decision. But first, grassroots leader from Pariabamba, explain. Why were small landowner's lands taken? Provincial Federation is authority of the province. Decision was only against gamonales, not small or medium landholders.

Delegate from Pariabamba: Masiykuna. It wasn't campesino group. It was government, with SINAMOS! Their promises to give away land have spread. Some confused people have believed them, they've taken over any old lands. But governments doesn't want to give land to campesinos. Just want to break unity of Provincial Federation. They want to make campesinos fight each other. That's why SINAMOS has taken land from small landowners. That's all.

Leader: Allinmi, compañerokuna.[44] Before we make a decision, we should say: We take over land from gamonales, land that has always belonged to us, all of us, from way back, our grandparents' land. Sometimes we have titles, but mistis never mind. Little by little, by cheating, by stealing, with money, with police, they've been taking from us. Hungry, exploited, we've suffered! Everything was and is abuse! They've even taken advantage of our women, and in some places, they still do! They get fat on our work, with our blood. That shouldn't happen! It can't keep happening! That's why we're against big guys, not against small landowners, like Mr. Dionisio Gonzales, here! In the struggle, we are learning that we should be united, no longer like little lambs on the loose. United with the small landowners, and mid-size, too, why not?! United in our decisions, in our actions, but united, through organization! In our Campesino Confederation of Peru, united in our Federation, in our organizations, just us campesinos. But important clarification is in order: We won't organize just to recover our land. No! Our struggle is to unite all campesino Peru Hatun Llaqta.[45] There's also city worker, factory worker, construction worker. There's also man dying of hunger in city, who doesn't have even half hectare of land, or house to live in. In hills, in sand dunes, they make huts of tin and reeds. Organized, they too are fighting. Organized, we too will unite with them, against all who make us suffer, against mistis! Against gringos! Against governments that have stained flag of Peru Hatun Llaqta! All united, like brothers, because we are brothers in misery-pain-hunger! Alone no more!

So, let's respect Dionisio Gonzales's small property. Those who agree, raise your hands . . .

Campesino 1: Huancahuacho, Lucrepata, Wankarama: agreed!

Campesino 2: Ongoy, Pacucha, Turpo, Pampachiri: fine!

Campesino 3: Kakiabamba, Cocharcas, Chincheros, Chiqmu: allinmi![46]

Campesino 4: Pariabamba, Sondondo, Acobamba: majority agrees!

Campesino 5: San Jerónimo, Lirkay, Uripa, Chaupiurqo: arí![47]

Campesino 6: Soraya, Andarapa, Chiara . . . agree (*Pauses*) But . . . Wankaray committee does not agree.

Leader: Tell us why.

Campesino 6: Arí, we will speak. Why will Dionisio Gonzales have land and not his workers? Why so much land just for him?

Leader: Suyaykuy![48] Wait, you will understand: in hillsides by Pariabamba hacienda, four hectares isn't much. There you can't produce like on level land, in valley with river water. They just hope for rain, there's no irrigation ditch. On coast, in other parts, four hectares is a lot. In hills, it's not much.

Another opinion? So, majority agrees. (*Addressing the small landowner*) You can go, no worries. (*To the assembly*) We will continue with assembly-tribunal . . .

Campesina: My problem, tayta . . .

The small landowner has not left.

Leader: What now?

Small landowner: I'm waiting for papers.

Leader: You want me to write?

Small landowner: Well, yes. If I say assembly decide, no one will believe me.

Leader: We'll make you a written mandate.

Small landowner: Yes, I want a decree.

Leader: We'll make a decree. Some committee leader, come up to sign.

Campesino: It should be Pariabamba leader . . . Tayta Pajares!

Committee leader Pajares approaches, greets the rest, looks at the pen doubtfully, and offers his index finger. The leader blots ink on the fingertip and takes his fingerprint. Pajares backs away, and the leader hands the decree to Gonzales.

Leader: Okay, now we will continue assembly . . .

Small landowner (*Returning*): This paper is worthless! It's signed with fingerprint! How can that be?

Leader: That's a leader's fingerprint, isn't it?

Small landowner: Yes, . . . yes, sure.

Leader: And leader represents the committee, doesn't he?

Small landowner: Yes, . . . yes, sure.

Leader: And what does the group say? It's going to make sure its decisions respected!

Larger group: Arí! Arí! . . . Yes, tayta, yes . . .

Leader: That's campesino justice!

Small landowner exits. At the same time, the campesino guard drags in Panchito Vega, who comes with a basket and a live hen.

Campesino Guard 1: Go on, go on, dammit! Let's see if you disrespect me in front of assembly!

Gregoria: There he is! That's Panchito Vega!

PANCHITO VEGA (*Approaching the leader*): Please accept these small tokens I've brought you. (*To the campesinos*) My children, I have come . . .

LEADER: Silence! Unless you have the floor, you don't talk! Señora Gregoria, approach, please. Speak.

GREGORIA: Should I tell truth?

LEADER: Arí!

GREGORIA: Hatun Asamblea, turíy![49] I have my husband. You know him . . . he is leader. I also have my little sheep. Just one, there's no money for more. You know what happened? Gamonal accused my husband of being thief. Says he has stolen sheep from hacienda! And that is a lie, brothers! Sheep has been mine always. Look at brand on his ear and you'll see. What happened is this Panchito Vega has lied to Gamonal. He is authority here, high authority, judge. And he is Gamonal's friend. Eats at his table, uses his spoon for soup, no doubt . . . Surely Gamonal told him: put Gregoria's husband in jail because he's bothering me . . . and so, with that thief-lie he jailed him. It's been a year already, . . . I demand justice! Give me back my husband . . . and my sheep, too . . .

LEADER (*To Panchito Vega*): You speak now.

PANCHITO VEGA: My children, how are you all? So pleased to be here. I have come here precisely of my own will, to clear up some misunderstandings. You all know me, and you know I am an honorable person, and I am not going to make problems for one sheep more or one sheep less . . .

GREGORIA: It's just one . . . My husband, why don't you talk about my husband!

PANCHITO VEGA: Regarding the situation of your husband, I would like to tell you, señora, with all the clarity that my good name demands, that you husband is no saint . . .

GREGORIA: And he's no thief, either! Why have you put him in jail? Tell me!

PANCHITO VEGA: I am a legal representative of justice in this country, appointed by the capital to serve my people in this small community, and therefore, my justice is blind . . .

GREGORIA: Hayayay! Your justice must be one-eyed. With your good eye, you look at boss, with your bad eye, at campesino . . .

PANCHITO VEGA: Señora, if you don't let me speak, we will not be able to converse like decent people . . .

GREGORIA: Well then, why don't you talk about my husband?

PANCHITO VEGA: Listen, Mr. Leader, why don't you tie up this cholita?[50] That way we can continue our dialogue . . . Well, my children, while they tie up this woman, I will tell you . . .

GREGORIA: What? You won't tie me up! Supay,[51] who do you think you are? Now you'll see.

Gregoria crosses over to where Vega is and attacks him while shouting.

Gregoria: Take that! Come on, say kawsachun![52] Long live the land takeovers! Rimayyá.[53]

The campesino guards enter to impose order and return Gregoria to her place. She is reprimanded by the leader.

Leader: Enough, Gregoria. Assembly is respect. Justice will be served!

Campesino: Floor, may I have the floor, leader? Thank you, wawqíy. Masiykuna![54] We are putting things in their place in our popular assembly. So, we need to see what people like this guy over there do. This man is not just taking advantage of his position as man of authority. No. As owner of large community store, too. We have no choice but to buy our things there. This man always greets us at the door like this: My boy! Have a little drink, and he gives us a lot of cañazo. Once he gets us drunk, you don't know what you're doing. And what happens? At the end of the month he gives us a list of things we haven't even bought. Besides, he's been tricking us, putting his thumb on the scales, our whole lives. All his products: candles, matches, whatever we need for cooking, everything, those thieves in ties from the capital are raising prices every day. And on top of that this man sells them to us for even more. How are we going to pay our debts? Since we don't have any money, this one starts taking our animals, starts taking our lands . . . I ask we annul all debts in the community. That we strip him of authority. That he return Gregoria's sheep. And her husband, well, we should get out of jail. Everyone.

LEADER (*To Panchito Vega*): You, speak.

PANCHITO VEGA: Thank you, Mr. Leader. I can't believe what I am hearing, my boy. What a sad life you have! How much hate you must have in that confused little head of yours! Such is life . . . One must be prepared for when some individual like him, at any moment, delivers a well-placed stab in the back! That's what our profession teaches us . . . because that's the way it is! . . . Weeds grow where no one plants them . . .

GREGORIA: Ha! You must be a tree, then.

PANCHITO VEGA: Just yesterday you came to my studio to ask me for favor, to say, Doctor, help me with this letter . . .

CAMPESINO: Forced to, I had no choice!

PANCHITO VEGA: . . . Can the doctor give me twenty-five-pound sack of salt, on credit . . . and you all know I am a good person. How many of you, hiding in the anonymity of this crowd, have come to ask me for help? I have always been happy to take care of you. But I came to this meeting prepared; my experience as a man of law has taught me these precautions. Here, on this paper, is the tally of what you and many of you owe me, you won't be able to deny it . . .

Leader gives a signal; a campesino guard grabs the paper from Panchito Vega. The Leader examines it, and slowly tears it up.

Gregoria: There are your lies.

The assembly praises these actions.

Panchito Vega (*Retrieving his gifts*): Damn gifts for another day . . . I'm leaving!

Leader: Not a step more! Campesino Guard! Now we're going to make decision. Popular assembly is law and order. And order is—first: we do not recognize authority of this man in community. Second: Señora Gregoria's sheep will be returned. And third, very important, we'll all go to jail to free Señora Gregoria's husband. Let Defense and Organization Committee be in charge of leading all the comuneros[55] in orderly fashion. That is the word!

All exit.

Leader (*Addressing the entire audience*): We should say that all we are doing, we can only do because we are

ORGANIZED! And now, just hold on a moment. While we're getting ready, let's bring in the Entertainment Committee. They are messengers of our feelings. Through the music and dance they perform for our pleasure, they show how our struggles have been, so that we never forget. And when they go to other places, they show what we are and what we are doing. They are our artists . . . (*Exits.*)

SEVEN
The Entertainment Committee

Enter three musicians; they place themselves to one side while to the beat of the music, from the opposite side, three couples of male and female campesinos enter performing the dance "Through the Andahuaylas Way" to an Andean bullfighting melody, "Peras Pispischay."

They enter dancing in pairs, celebrating the takeover. Two women pull over a campesino to disguise him as a gamonal. He resists but eventually accepts, and the female campesinos dress him in boots, leather jacket, mask and hat, and leave him in the middle of the stage, while returning to dance. The disguised campesino takes on the role of the gamonal and dances contemptuously. He forces the campesinos to follow him. Then he separates the partners. He orders them to go from one side to another and afterwards relegates them to the back of the stage; meanwhile, facing the audience, he dances in triumph. In the back, the campesinos dance disorderedly. At that moment a campesino enters dancing with the Peruvian flag and a red chullo;[56] *they then dance in orderly fashion, surrounding the "gamonal" and kicking him out. They force him to climb a pole; making fun of him, they push him to spin him around. Enter another campesino dressed as a soldier, dancing with martial arts-style leaps. The campesinos throw out the "gamonal." With this, he tears the Peruvian flag from the hands of the Leader and begins to dance with different military-like steps, trying to involve each of the campesinos one by one. Some follow him, no longer dancing as they were, and they change their dance steps.*

The group of campesinos that remains next to the leader begins to dance with force calling to the others to return to their first dance. They return and recover the flag.

Campesino (*Interrupting the dance*): Masiykuna, they're sending word that they have recognized our leader by his pukachullo[57] and are trying to take him away!

Confusion.

Campesina: The police! Ayáw . . . ay . . . (*She runs away.*)

Another campesina: Oh, oh, where are you going? Stay here, dammit!

Others: What should we do? They want to take him. We need to protect him.

LEADER: Calm down, llaqta masiykuna.[58] Who are there more of here?

ALL: Us!

LEADER: And who is in charge, dammit!

ALL: Campesinokuna!!!![59]

LEADER: Well, then, comuneros, let the Campesino Guard be in charge of going out with the Defense Committees, surrounding the hills. And we, masiykuna, will keep dancing, with the strength of Indians, all night long! Wifala![60]

They all return to the dance. The campesinos protect the leader and take him to the back. They all surround him, dancing, and all sing this song while showing signs of strength and bravery. They go about passing around the leader's pukachullo and dancing with it on. All sing.

31 de agostotas, peras pispischay[61]
gamonalta qarqurqanchik, peras pispischay
Gamolanpa wasinpiqa, peras pispischay.
Campesino tiyaykuchkan, peras pispischay.
Gamonalpa platunpiqa, peras pispischay
Campesino mikuychkan, peras pispischay.
Gamonalpa camanpiqa, peras pispischay.
Campesino puninkuchkan, peras pispichay
Gamonalpa warmintaqa, peras pispichay
Campesino awkikuchkan, peras pispichay.[62]

All exit dancing, following the Peruvian flag. A campesina remains on stage.

EIGHT
The Testimony

GREGORIA: Well, brother, that's how we began to laugh. Mamáy, maqtacha,[63] child, that's the way it was, how we found our feet along the way. How we recovered lands in our community over there in Andahuaylas. Years and years, we've felt the boss's beatings on our bodies, because we were like loose little stones. We were only freed of our anger when our chests became bitter and we sang:

Kay Perú nacionpi, hambre miseria
manaña tukuq
Ay haykapkamaraq
wakchalla kasun
pobrella kasun
Kay Perú nacionpi
Campesino runa hatarillasunña
vamos a la lucha
Ay haykapkamaraq
wakchalla kasun
gamonalista sirvispa.[64]

That was how we shared our feelings. But that feeling grew and grew like flood trying to drown us. And fighting for land, that anger exploded like raging river that sweeps away and destroys everything. Because of that struggle we were no longer the same; we have felt different. Surely you will not understand what it is to always love the land, and for it to reek, as if filled with salt. Could you understand what it is then to plant seeds for everyone, and feel that the recovered land no longer weeps or hates anyone? To plant like that . . . like that . . . placing new seed, ours now, and watch it grow up green. We watered it with care, softly, caressing so it grew well. Surely you won't understand what it is to always view boss's house like ghost house, head bowed, his ugly voice hurting your ears, so you can't think. Do you know what it is to enter that house that we never knew without touching our forehead to the ground? Its floor was shiny, like a mirror. We touched everything, his spoon, his plate, his clothes, what big beds! Do you know what it is to do all that and not be afraid? (*Pauses*). Or when we held popular tribunal! Misti laws have never been for campesinos. That's why we made Popular Trial. We told it like it was, calmly we said what we were thinking. To governments, too.

(*Singing*)

Lima capitalpi, cojo Velasco[65]
Llapan llaqtapi SINAMOS

Dulces palabras, negra conciencia
wakcha runata engañan.[66]

Because many brothers had been fooled. They believed false words, they believed it, that the Agrarian Reform was revolution . . . But we didn't kick them out, go on, shoo, here no more. We didn't allow tricks. We called them: paníy, turíy, little brother, papáy, mamáy, wawqíy, father,[67] who killed your brother? Who spilled blood soaking our land?! Who sent policiachapas[68] with weapons that, bang, spit fire? It was government with lying words. Well, then, who are you going to believe? That's how we spoke, and many understood. Why let ourselves be killed? We, carrying liwis, warakas,[69] sticks, stones; they, with the weapons they have that let them keep lying. We won't let this happen anymore. No more believing governments of false wiraqochas[70] with lying words. Should campesino always stay quiet? Campesino has always fought, not just in Andahuaylas. And I who am speaking to you, I'm not only campesina from Andahuaylas; I'm also campesina from Qosqollay, from Cajamarca am I, from Piura, from Lambayeque, from all Peru Hatun Llaqta am I campesina,[71] and I'm here to tell you how we are living, how we have learned that we should be united like this . . . like this with man from city, with you. Light has dawned among us. Through shouts and cries it grew. Piercing stones of mountains, the light is reaching all corners, so it will never fade (*Pauses*). It is dawning. Taytacha sol,[72] his head is appearing over the hilltops, coloring the air of these lands . . .

(Singing)

Campesino obrero alianakusunchik[73]
vamos a la lucha,
vamos a la lucha definitiva
hasta conseguir la liberación.[74]

NINE
The Women's Committee

Pastora (*Entering*): Yaw, tiyáy . . . imaynalla kachkanki . . .[75] What were you doing?

Gregoria: . . . I was planting . . . What are you doing? Why are you carrying instruments?

Pastora: Auntie, have you forgotten, there's women's meeting; Campesino Guard is coming.

Gregoria: Oh, darn, I had forgotten! We must have Women's Committee meeting for welcoming. Come, you help me (*They start to leave*). What can we give them?

Pastora: A little chicha[76] . . .

Gregoria: . . . and some toasted corn with kachikurpa![77]

Georgina appears on opposite side.

GEORGINA: Oh, there come Gregoria and Pastora . . . I bet they're coming to take me to Women's Committee meeting, they won't stop bugging me . . . what can I say to them this time?

She runs to one side to hide.

PASTORA: Look, Auntie, Georgina saw us from afar, and she's gone hiding like scared sheep.

GREGORIA: Yes, I see her . . . I bet she doesn't want to go to women's meeting. Let's go down this path.

PASTORA: Yes, let's go.

Realizing she's been caught, Georgina pretends to cry.

GREGORIA: Hey, Georgina, how are you . . . ?

GEORGINA: Imaynalla kachkanki, mamacha,[78] how are you Pastora?

GREGORIA: What has you crying like that, like caged dog?

GEORGINA: It's my wawita,[79] he has fever, and so much diarrhea . . . I don't have time for anything . . .

GREGORIA: Give me child, I'll cure him.

GEORGINA (*Getting up quickly*): No mamacha, I'm just in a hurry, with coca tea, with horsetail tea, he'll be fine, I'm in a hurry, mamita, I'm going.

Pastora (*Catching up to her*): Wait, it would be better to give him to my auntie, she knows how to cure wawas.[80]

Gregoria: Here, let's see (*She takes the baby*). Pastora, what do you think? Maybe someone cast him evil eye . . .

Pastora (*Looking at his face*): Oooohh, his little face is green . . .

Gregoria: Maybe he's dying . . .

They both look at Georgina, who is becoming frightened.

Gregoria: Liar! . . . Why are you telling lies? Look at his little face, nice and rosy.

Georgina: Give me back my child . . . as if he were yours! I have a lot to do; I'd better be going!

Gregoria: Wait. We have an invitation for you! Campesino Guard is coming and all us women have to prepare reception.

Pastora: Yes! Campesino Guard will talk to all the community youth . . .

Georgina: Ah, I've heard all communities are coming down, there's going to be big party, isn't there?

Gregoria and **pastora:** Come on then, let's get to work!

Georgina: Ay, I can't go. I need to take Hugo to school, he's just six years old. He has to walk so far . . .

Pastora: My little brother, younger than Hugo and goes all by himself!

Georgina: But I also have to cook, I have to wash, I have to take care of animals . . . there's no time . . . !

Pastora: And I, too, have my guinea pigs, my chickens . . .

Gregoria: And I, too, have lots to cook, for eight children and then more for my husband, and I'm going to meeting. Why aren't you going?

Pastora (*Secretly*): Auntie, could it be that her husband won't let her go?

Georgina (*Who has heard her*): No, lies! Julián hasn't said anything to me.

Gregoria: Ay, would that I were you! I've had so many fights with my husband . . . we've gone head to head until I've convinced him, I have right to go to meeting. I even invited him. And I go because I like to, wouldn't you?

Georgina (*Who has been listening attentively, begins to cry*): I would like to, mamita, . . . but if I go, my husband will beat me.

Gregoria: He beats you? How do you allow that, Georgina? You have to use your mouth, talk to him, you have to say what you think. What, are you his enemy, is that why he hits you?

Georgina: He doesn't listen to me . . . he won't even look at the children . . . And if I go to meeting maybe he'll get even more angry . . . But I want to go, big, nice party . . . Why don't you come with me to talk to my husband?

Gregoria: No, he's your husband. You have to go by yourself to talk and make decision. Come with us now! And later, if he beats you again, we'll go with delegation, more women and men, to talk to your husband!

Georgina: And what can I do with the wawas, how can I leave them alone?

Pastora: Bring them with you! All the women take their children, and we make big meal together.

Gregoria: Stop crying, now! Let's get your wawas and go to meeting!

Pastora, Georgina, Gregoria: Come on, let's go!

A Campesino appears.

Campesino: Doña Gregoria . . . Georgina! Campesino Guard is coming, through the ravine. They're walking strong.

Gregoria and **Pastora:** Oh, oh, oh, let's go. Bring instrument, for welcoming.

They prepare to welcome the Campesino Guard.

TEN

The Campesino Guard

Dance of the campesinos in charge of defense and discipline in the takeovers. Shouts of joy and strength. Enter the Campesino Guard carrying ropes, liwis, warakas. To the music of Dance of the Tucumanos, the guard performs a dance that exalts the valor, strength, and courage of the campesino. Finally, after some energetic maneuvers, they exit, galloping. The women exit behind them. The guards yell "Allpanchik Rayku Runakuna"[81] *and other cheers.*

ELEVEN

Towards Power

Enter all campesinos quickly. They erupt on stage, one of them carrying the Tawantisuyu flag. The leader carries the Peruvian flag, and they form the same scene with which the play opened.

One campesino: Here I am!
Campesinas: Strengthened by your blood!
Campesinos: Not dead . . . !
All: Still shouting!!!

They exit to the rhythm of the tarkas, pututos[82] *and shouting.*

TWELVE

Like a Fiesta in the Country

When the play seems to be finished, a bugle sounds, and campesinos appear playing Spanish-style music that will accompany the entrance of the bullfighter. Behind the bullfighter enter two manolas,[83] *also wearing masks, who stay behind the bullfighter, egging him on.*

Suddenly the campesinos change the music and play on zampoñas and bombo[84] *the music of the Wakawaka*[85] *or Dance of the Bullpen, and a campesino, wearing a bull costume, enters dancing.*

They perform a dance that symbolizes a bullfight with all of its vicissitudes, in burlesque style. Finally, the bullfighter is conquered and killed by the bull. The manolas rush to help him, and the bull finishes them off. Everyone invites the audience to dance, accompanied by firecrackers and huaynos.

END

Notes

1. Túpac Amaru I was the last Incan monarch under Spanish rule. Born in 1545, thirteen years after the conquest of Peru, he was executed by the Spaniards in 1572. His descendent, Túpac Amaru II (born José Gabriel Condorcanqui) led a series of unsuccessful Indigenous rebellions against the Spaniards in the eighteenth century. Túpac Amaru II was brutally executed along with his family members and other rebel

leaders on 18 May 1781. He remains an iconic figure of Andean resistance to this day.

2. *Tarka*—a wooden Andean flute with a mouthpiece, six finger holes, and an open hole at the end. *Tarola*—snare drum made of wood, goatskin, and string snares.

3. This rainbow-striped flag, currently the flag of Cuzco, is used in contemporary times to represent the Tawantinsuyo, or Incan Empire, as well as Andean Indigenous identity and resistance broadly speaking.

4. Located in the Department of Cuzco, the snowcapped Salqantay mountain is considered an *apu*, or deity, by local Indigenous communities.

5. The play opens with the first lines of "Tupac Amaru kamaq taytanchisman," perhaps the most famous Quechua poem by the renowned neo-Indigenist creative writer and anthropologist José María Arguedas (see the introduction for more information on Arguedas's deep influence in the Yuyachkani corpus). In this citation, Arguedas's original spelling has been maintained. Otherwise, in the rest of the play, the Quechua orthography has been regularized to reflect the collaboration and interplay of Chanka and Cuzco Quechua speakers behind the creation of the plays.

6. *Taytáy*—my father; *Mamáy*—my mother; terms of respect and endearment that can been used with male and female adults, respectively.

7. *Gamonal*—large landowner. *Gamonalismo* refers to the semi-feudal system that governed the Andes until the Agrarian Reform of the 1960s. Within this system, an extension of the colonial Spanish *encomienda*, an estate granted to Spanish colonizers, the *gamonal* had complete authority over the Indigenous peoples living in the hacienda lands. The system was denounced by early Indigenist writers, including Mariátegui.

8. *Guagua*—child; *guaguita*—little child (from Quechua *wawa*, child of a woman; *ushi* and *churi* are used to refer, respectively, to a daughter and son of a man).

9. *Jajaylas*—a Quechua expression of disgust or anger.

10. *Waqra phuku*—a trumpet made of a hollowed bull's horn.

11. *Cholo*—In the Andes, a derogatory term for Indigenous or Indigenous-mestizo people.

12. "Carnival of '74 / you came here / to gather, to unite / the Andahualyas campesinos. / These / campesinos you assembled / growing large and gathering strength / from these lands / have banished gamonal / In Huancahuacho hacienda / in Toxama hacienda / the evil owl

is singing / the gamonal's death / foretelling. / Because you've been exploiter / Because you've been dominator / death's caught you by surprise / that's why the bells / are ringing out your death."

13. *Cañazo*—alcoholic sugar cane beverage, like *aguardiente*. This is the chorus of the Andean *huayno* "15 de julio," by Lino Quintanilla (1975), in homage to the takeover of the Wankawachu hacienda in Andahuaylas; Buleje and Vergara, historical figures, were managers of the hacienda.

14. SINAMOS—Sistema Nacional de Apoyo a la Movilización Social, or National System for the Support of Social Mobilization, was created in 1971 by the government of Juan Velasco Alvarado to encourage the development of grassroots organizations to resolve social problems and buttress support for the government. Many campesinos experienced SINAMOS as yet another intrusion by outside, government forces.

15. *Waraka*—sling.

16. "They say that on the 15th of July / we took back our Huancahuacho lands / Little gamonales, little policemen / can't touch us campesinos. / For a few coins / the gamonales made us work / Where is their exploitation now? / We disappeared it forever. / With our lives or with our deaths / we will defend our land / even as we spill our blood / we campesinos will fight forever. / (*Fugue*) / Cañazo de Huancahuacho / relieve my anger / I'm so furious at the gamonal / at SINAMOS / Qollpakuchu orange / refresh my heart / for I am enraged at Vergara / at Buleje / This is our coming and going / This is our arriving / And I do have my sling / And I do have my sword / I don't care if it's someone I love / I don't care if it's someone I embrace / To the one saying, 'Stop, brother,' / I'll throw you in the river / I'll shove you into the abyss."

17. *Andahuaylina*—woman from Andahuaylas.

18. "Hey you, not worthy of love."

19. "Hey, these sacks are all torn; where could the needle be? Ah, here it was. Now, I'll get going to work."

20. "Pastorita (*dim.*), hey, come here, listen. We're going to the farm. No one's there. Hurry, Pastora."

21. "Hey, go away, my mother could arrive."

22. "No, no one's here. We're alone."

23. "Hey, go on, our group leader could come. We must work, I have to sew."

24. "Tomorrow we'll get up early to sew. Come on."

25. "No."

26. "Let's drink."
27. "Here's some toasted corn snack, young lady, let's eat."
28. "Fellow campesinos!"
29. "What!"
30. "Yes."
31. "Yes, sir!"
32. "Over here, grand leader!"
33. "Good!"
34. "We're here!"
35. "Everyone's here!"
36. *Colonos*—peasants tied to a specific hacienda.
37. "Be quiet!"
38. *Misti*—term used to refer to members of the local upper or ruling classes in the Andes.
39. *Qanqaruna*—Nasal-voiced, stutterer (an insult in the Ayacucho region).
40. "I will speak. Friends, what are we doing fighting among ourselves like cats and dogs? That's not good, we need to be very, very careful. Is that what we're going to teach our children? No. Or are we fools?"
41. "Let him speak."
42. "Speak . . . my brother."
43. "Show me your hands!"
44. *Compañerokuna*—"Friends" (or "comrades"). Note the Quechua plural suffix, *-kuna*, combined with the Spanish *compañero* ("comrade").
45. *Hatun Llaqta*—"The whole nation" (or "great town").
46. "Good!"
47. "Yes!"
48. "Wait!"
49. "Great Assembly, my brother!"
50. *Cholita*—Spanish, pejorative term for Indigenous people or mestizos.
51. "Devil."
52. "Long live."
53. "Say it already."
54. "Thank you, brothers. Comrades!"
55. *Comuneros*—a general term for members of independent Indigenous communities, or *ayllus*.
56. *Chullo*—A typical wool hat from the Andean region.
57. *Pukachullo*—Red chullo hat.
58. *Masiykuna*—Fellow townspeople.

59. "The campesinos!"

60. *Wifala*—An expression of celebration and encouragement, like "Hooray!" Here, Yuyachkani takes some liberties, as the expression is not generally used in western Apurímac, where the play takes place.

61. *Peras piquichay*—a nonsensical phrase that helps maintain the rhythm and rhyme of the song. *Pispis* or *pispischa* is a girl's game similar to jacks, in which the girls must complete complicated clapping rhythms before picking up their piece. *Pispis* can also be used to indicate something insignificant or virtually nonexistent, such as "He doesn't know *pispis*."

62. "On 31 August / We threw out the gamonal / In the house of the gamonal / The campesino took control / From the plates of the gamonal / The campesino's eating now / In the bed of the gamonal / The campesino's sleeping now / And the wife of the gamonal / The campesino's enjoying now."

63. *Maqtacha*—young man.

64. "In this country Peru, / Hunger and misery always / Oh! How long will we be / Poor? / Will we be poor? / In this Peru, / Campesinos all, rise up! / Onward to the fight / Oh, how long will we be / Poor / Serving the gamonal? / Campesinos all, rise up! / Onward to the fight / Oh, how long will we be / Poor / Serving the gamonal?"

65. Towards the end of his regime Velasco fell very ill and his right leg was amputated, hence the reference to his being "lame." By 1973, a devastating economic recession meant that he was unpopular even among the peasants he had helped free from the hacienda regime in the Agrarian Reform of 1969.

66. In the capital Lima, lame Velasco / In all the towns, SINAMOS / Sweet words, black soul, / They fool the poor.

67. "Sister, brother, mother, father . . ."

68. "Who sent the police even."

69. *Liwi*—a traditional weapon made of a cord with smaller cords at each end, often used to catch animals. The smaller cords have small rocks or metal balls affixed to their ends. *Waraka*—sling.

70. *Wiraqocha*—used by Andean Indigenous peasants to refer to powerful whites or mestizos. The term comes from the Andean creation deity, Wiraqocha or Viracocha, which Indigenous peoples began to associate with Spaniards during the conquest.

71. *Qosqollay*—my beloved Cuzco; *Hatun Llaqta*—nation (or "great town"). Here, the woman claims to represent all campesinos throughout Peru.

72. "Father sun"

73. "Let's unite." Note that *alianakusunchik* uses the Spanish base *aliarse* ("to unite") with the Quechua reciprocal and verb conjugation suffixes.

74. Campesino and worker, let's unite / Let's go to the fight / To the final fight / Until we are free.

75. "Hey, Auntie . . . How are you?"

76. *Chicha*—fermented corn beer.

77. *Kachikurpa*—a salty cheese.

78. "How are you, ma'am?"

79. "Child."

80. "Children."

81. "This is for our land, people!"

82. *Pututo*—A large shell instrument of pre-Hispanic origin, used as a ceremonial trumpet and to call meetings.

83. *Manola*—a stereotypical Spanish woman, generally dressed in a traditional black or colorful dress and a mantilla.

84. *Zampoña*—a traditional Andean pan flute; *bombo*—traditional drum made of a hollowed tree trunk and topped with a cured animal skin.

85. *Wakawaka*—"cow-cow," from the Spanish "vaca-vaca," referring to the calls made to taunt a bull.

Against-the-Wind (1985)

Against-the-Wind tells the story of Machula and his two daughters, Coya and Huaco, who, driven from their home by the violence and death wrought by the Internal Armed Conflict, set out in search of the "seeds of life."[1] The story is narrated by an *equeqo*, an Andean good luck spirit, and includes characters from the festival of the Virgin of Candelaria in Paucartambo (in Cuzco Province): el Arcángel ("Archangel"), la China Diabla ("China"), and el Caporal ("Caporal").[2] These festival characters, traditionally Indigenous mockings of the colonial Spaniards, represent the forces that fueled the rural violence during the early days of the Shining Path conflict, wiping out entire towns in their death raids. The two sisters, Coya and Huaco (whose names are drawn from Andean mythology) represent two alternatives of the response to that violence: Huaco goes out to join the fighting, and Coya heads to the coast to seek justice through the courts. The play develops in what Yuyachkani terms a "registro mítico" ("mythic register"; Rubio Zapata 105; my trans.); highly symbolic, it contains many specialized cultural references, and does not decidedly align itself with either side of the Internal Armed Conflict, though the heavier dramatic treatment given to Coya might suggest a preference for a pacifistic response to the violence.

Against-the-Wind is dedicated to the historian Alberto Flores Galindo, author of *Buscando un Inca: Identidad y utopía en los Andes* (*In Search of an Inca: Identity and Utopia in the Andes*), who, says director Miguel Rubio Zapata, "habló de la utopía andina . . . para repensar el futuro, es decir, construir un discurso que él llama la dimensión utópica del hombre andino, pero no entendiéndolo como ese hombre estático . . . al margen de cualquier tipo de modernidad, sino como un hombre que está generando cultura" ("spoke of an Andean utopia . . . in order to rethink the future, that is, to construct a discourse that he called the utopic dimension of the Andean man, but not understanding him as that static man . . . at the margin of any form of modernity, but as a man generating culture"; 105; my trans.). Flores Galindo proposes that "la utopía andina no es únicamente un esfuerzo por entender el pasado o por ofrecer una alternativa al presente. Es también un intento de vislumbrar el futuro. Tiene esas tres dimensiones" ("the Andean Utopia has three dimensions: not only does it attempt to understand the past or provide an alternative to the present, but it also seeks to discern the future"; *Buscando* 59; *In Search of an Inca* 48–49). This concept vastly opens up theatrical and theoretical possibilities for the group and prompts a deeper exploration of myth as a cultural and political element.

A video of a performance of the play is available in the online digital library of the Hemispheric Institute (Grupo Cultural Yuyachkani).

Notes

1. Each character name has a cultural significance. *Machula* means "grandfather," "ancestor," or "old man" in Quechua, though here he is the father of Coya and Huaco. *Coya* (or, *quya*, in standardized Quechua) was the name given to the wife of the Inca, the highest-ranking woman in the Incan empire. *Huaco* refers to Mama Huaco, one of the early Incan Coyas, said to have given maize to the Andean peoples and to have conquered the Sacred Valley of Cuzco. She has a decidedly warrior-like, masculine character and is associated with infertility.

2. All three characters are key players in the *Diablada*, or Dance of the Demons, in the Festival of the Virgin of Candelaria in Puno. The China Diabla is a beautiful and evil female figure charged with taunting the Archangel, who is defending the Virgin (*china* refers to a female animal in Quechua, and *diabla* means "devil" in Spanish). A symbol of evil femininity, La China is sometimes portrayed as the wife of the Caporal, who represents colonial viceregal aristocracy. The Arcángel (Archangel Michael) is normally portrayed as defending peace, but in this play he is aligned with the forces of evil.

Works Cited

Flores Galindo, Alberto. *Buscando un Inca: Identidad y utopía en los Andes*. 4th ed., Editorial Horizonte, 1984.

———. *In Search of an Inca: Identity and Utopia in the Andes*. Translated and edited by Carlos Aguirre et al., Cambridge UP, 2010.

Grupo Cultural Yuyachkani. *Contraelviento*. Directed by Miguel Rubio Zapata, 1996. *Hemispheric Institute*, hemisphericinstitute.org/en/hidvl-collections/item/128-yuya-contralviento.html.

Rubio Zapata, Miguel. *Notas sobre el teatro*. Edited by Luis A. Ramos-García, Grupo Cultural Yuyachkani, 2001.

Character List

In order of appearance:

EQUEQO

MACHULA

HUACO

COYA

THE CAPORAL

THE ARCHANGEL

THE CHINA DIABLA

THE JUDGE

THE SCRIBE

ONE

Hanaq Pacha[1]

The hills sing "Hanaq Pachap Kusikuynin."[2]

Hanaq pachap kusikuynin
Waranqakta much'asqayki
Yupay ruru puquq mallki
Runakunap suyakuynin
Kallpannaqpa q'imikuynin
Waqyasqayta.
Uyariway much'asqayta
Diospa rampan Diospa maman
Yuraq tuqtu hamanq'ayman

Yupasqalla, qullpasqayta
Wawaykiman suyusqayta
Rikuchillay.[3]

The Equeqo[4] *appears; the hills rise up. A woman emerges and gives the Equeqo a small bag.*

EQUEQO: This maize was given to me by a woman who, coming out of the hills, told me the story that I now bring to you.

TWO
The First Table

The hills rise, and Coya falls. Machula performs a ritual cleansing of the air and of Coya while she sings.

MACHULA: Coya, my daughter, what are you seeing? What about your dreams make you wish not to wake?

HUACO: It's been three days and three nights already, Papáy.[5] She hasn't wanted to eat at all.

MACHULA: It was necessary, Huaco. This way, her spirit is strengthened; her dream will soon tell us something.

He keeps singing softly, while Coya, half awake, half asleep, rises and begins to speak.

Coya: Papáy . . . I dreamed there was a lone mountain and night was falling. A very old man, with a sad face and clothes soaked in bright blood, appeared to me . . . "Hide!" he said. "They're coming . . ." And they appeared from two sides. Some advanced hungrily, breathing their last. With their large hands, they tossed cows, calves, seeds, and other things into the air, devouring everything to calm their hunger. Others, also hungry, came hurling houses and roofs through the air, destroying everything, like the first ones, leaving nothing for us. And, in the middle of it all, there we were, not knowing what to do, out in the open . . . machetes and axes, knives and flints whizzed by, like in a dance, looking for something to slice . . . when all of a sudden, I saw that the mountain range and the sea merged, as if boiling, and that it wasn't water flowing out, but a foul-smelling substance, like fat, like oil, covering the earth and leaving her sterile, dry, wrinkled . . . We ran from one side to another, looking for some pretty colored stones among the dry cracks. We danced; at times, we also laughed. Then, in a hurry, we again looked for those little stones; they were very important for . . . I don't remember, I don't remember. There were hundreds of men and women walking with their eyes cast down, hiding their faces. They slipped away into the cracks. There were no more bodies; there was not one single body left on the face of the earth. I saw all of that in my dream, and I also saw that you two were no longer with me.

She falls down again and tries to go back to sleep.

MACHULA: Now, I remember the old wise man, the Yachaq,[6] when he said to a poor woman from the highlands: The two fox sons growing in your womb will devour the whole world in one day and one night. So the woman fled . . . the woman, like any other woman, suffered and gave birth. She then saw that the black fox went towards the mountains, gobbling up the towns of this world, the rich ones of ancient times. The white fox dove into the sea. He, too, went about eating people and making men flee as they turned to stone . . . Only one man survived, and he arrived at the Lauricocha puna[7] where the foxes were. Upon seeing them, the man lay down and pretended to sleep. The foxes talked among themselves: "Brother, we've finished off this world; another one will begin, it will be with white men. They will have to suffer and toil to be able to eat. Now let's drink some water, brother . . ." And as they were drinking, the man rose up and plunged them deep into the water. To this day they can be found in the lake, the two foxes. If one day they are able to escape, the world will end . . . [8] Coya, daughter, stop dreaming. Huaco, daughter, calm down. Those colored stones you see in your dreams are the maize of life being destroyed. Your dream also tells me that before it's too late we should go out and search for the best seeds of maize to plant. We'll go from town to town. They must be hidden.

Coya: Don't worry, Papáy . . . don't be afraid, dear sister.

Machula: We won't hide anymore.

Huaco: And, then, where will we go?

Machula: I don't know right now, I just know we should follow the orders of the Yachaq and leave soon to search for the maize of life.

Coya: Yes, but very soon. I feel our time is short.

They begin their journey. A malignant wind appears, destroying everything and abducting Coya. Machula resists, confronting the wind with his sacred vara[9] *to protect Huaco. He is wounded.*

Machula: Asta ya, suwa runa, supay wayrakuna ripuychik, parapis manan atinqakuchu.[10]

The wind disappears.

Huaco: Papáy, millay wayrakuna apakum ñañayta. Kunanqa sapallanchik, kachkanchik waqaspa, imapaqmi suyamuranchik kunankama.[11]

Machula tries to get up and run.

Machula: Run, go look for your sister, do this for me. Maybe the wayra[12] released her! But hide if you see the dust rise up!

They exit. The Equeqo appears.

Equeqo: I forgot to tell you that hundreds of years ago the gods of the earth and the heavens gave me powers.

Music. Equeqo dances.

Equeqo: That is why I can move mountains, dry up rivers, grant wishes to people. Strange things have been happening for years now. People come and tell me, "He went that way, he was happy, but still I want him back. Bring him back to me!" And, bam! Others come and tell me "The Wayra, the evil wind, took him." Just like Coya!

THREE
The Dance

The Archangel and China enter dancing with Coya, who does not know where she is. Throughout the entire scene, the Archangel and China speak to Coya using steps, gestures, and sounds, falsely convincing her that they are her saviors and that she should cure the Caporal.

Archangel and China move about making noise.

Coya: Yes, I wanted to keep dancing to forget my troubles. Perhaps I am already in my people's heaven, and this is how you welcome me . . . But, no, it can't be . . . I'm alive; you've saved me!

Music. The Archangel, Coya, and China spin around.

Coya: The evil wind dragged me away, you two appeared and snatched me back from him . . . How was that possible? Are you really so strong? (*To the Archangel*) Was it you? (*To China*) Was it you?

Music. China moves about making noise.

Coya: Ah . . . It was your boss, the Caporal! . . . How I would love to see him, and thank him for saving my life!

The Archangel and China talk among themselves, climbing over each other and carrying each other around.

China moves about making noise.

Coya: Sick? What kind of illness can someone who confronts such an evil wind have?

China moves about making noise.

Coya: Yes, that's true . . . I know about plants, and my eyes see beyond the shadows. But I don't want to, I can't cure him . . .

The Archangel and China threaten her softly.

Archangel moves about making noise.

Coya (*Worried*): Fine. If you're going to ask like that . . . bring him over, and I'll get started.

Coya sets up her mesa.[13] *She sings. The Caporal starts to enter on the back of the China Diabla. The Archangel makes way for him. Coya sees him and is briefly afraid. Then, she resumes setting up.*

Coya: I see you are suffering greatly, sir. Rest assured, I'll help you. Looking inside you, I see something very strong, growing, consuming, a bright light that is eating you up . . . right here, through your foot! That must be why your legs are so tiny. Take this black stone in your hand, hold it tightly, like this (*She performs a ritual cleansing*). Now, go ahead, speak! Let everything go! Have confidence! Let the bad go and the good in! Kick, stomp, hard, light up the floor! You are rising, you are becoming yourself, sir, ay ay ay . . .

The Caporal recovers, and is now larger and has all of his horns. Coya quickly gathers her objects, with growing fear.

Coya: You must be feeling better now, sir. Someone is harming you; someone doesn't want you to reap what you

Coya (left) heals the Caporal. Photograph by Miguel Villafañe.

are sowing—I don't know what it is. I'm going to give you a charm so you can protect yourself. You just have to pay attention to what I am telling you now, do you understand? Now, you must forgive me because I have to go . . . I don't know what happened to my sister, to my tayta[14] . . . My path is that way! Ay! Let me go, let me go!

The Caporal, the Archangel, and China whisk her up in their dance and take her away. They dance with the wind.

FOUR
The War

Equeqo: And so, while the Archangel and China wrapped Coya up in their joyful dances, Huaco searched for her sister in the mountain: "Coya! Coyacha!"

Huaco: Coya, Coyacha, Coyacháy! Maypim kachkanki? Maypim chinkapunki ñañáy?[15]

The Archangel and China enter, inspecting the area, then they move about destroying everything in their path, and finally, the Caporal enters, triumphant. They dance and play bugles triumphantly. The Archangel and China exit while the Caporal remains dancing in a corner. Huaco has witnessed everything.

Huaco: I went, running, running, from one town to another. They were all empty, but there were signs that terrible things had happened. Atop a mountain I could see a small town far off in a great cloud of dust. I ran down the mountain and hiding behind a stone I could see them.

The Archangel and China enter dragging a large bundle. The Caporal, Archangel, and China exit while Huaco remains spinning around on stage.

HUACO: They were monstrous beings, with immense archangel wings and demonic faces. People ran about terrified, as if they had seen the devil. That's how it was. They had an immense pot. They were dragging people, dragging them by the hair to the top of the church, and from there, they threw the people into the pot to turn them to old, wrinkled flesh.

The father enters and listens to his daughter Huaco's story.

. . . in the middle of it all there was a woman. I thought it was Coya. Arí, yes, it was her. Papáy, I saw how those monstrous beings were killing, and I haven't been able to do anything but cry and scream in horror.

MACHULA (*Giving the vara to Huaco*): Sayariy, get up, keep telling me. I need to know.

HUACO: Arí, Papáy. I remember now. The biggest one of all, the most beautiful and horrible, dressed in brilliant white, with immense horns, opened his gold and silver cape and grabbed that little woman, my sister, and forced himself on her. Then, she was snatched from the earth by angels and archangels and by devils with goat legs, that took her flying up to the top of the church and then threw her off . . . I wanted to do something, but the dust and the wind enveloped everything. When I could see again, the town was empty. They had taken all the bodies away, even Coya's.

MACHULA: No! Coya's not dead, she's alive somewhere. I feel her heart; I feel her breath. Now it's even more necessary to be together and to go out in search of the maize of life.

HUACO: I've seen so much death, and you ask me to go look for the seeds of life. Coya's dream has become a reality! It's being fulfilled! Papáy, give me your strength; I want to go fight them.

MACHULA: If you had seen and lived what I have, you would understand things differently.

HUACO: I'm not waiting any longer. For Coya, my dear sister, ñañáy,[16] like the black fox, I will climb the mountains.

MACHULA: If that is your last word, then go, run, fly, find what you are looking for.

The father hands her a black mask, and they dance.

MACHULA: If you leave, come back just as you are now; do not come back in spirit.

They finish dancing, and Huaco leaves, while Machula is attacked by evil winds. He fights them, conquers them, and ascends to the Apus.[17]

FIVE
The Table of the Damned

MACHULA: I am here before you again to ask you all for help, at this moment, when the night grows darker.

(Singing)

Qamraykutaq hukmanta hamuni
Kikillan ñawpaq hinaraq
Yanapawanaykichikpaq
Chisip tukunan pacha
Chayrayku apamuyki aswan allin wayta
 tarisqay
Umayta kikin kasqanta churapuwaychik
Ñawiy allin rikurinanpaq[18]

What a profound silence! Where are the seeds we are seeking? I can't find them. Could this be the end of mankind and life?

Machula hears a groan that comes from afar. He sees the bundle, opens it, and Coya appears.

MACHULA: Coya, daughter.

COYA: Papáy.

MACHULA: Kaypimá kachkasqanki, wawalláy,[19] but who did that to you, my child?

COYA: I don't know, Papáy. I don't know how much time has passed since they put me away in here . . .

MACHULA: Since the evil wind snatched you, I've been searching for you, with so much sorrow in my heart. I've faced the wind again, but I don't know who sends it.

COYA: The evil wind . . . Someone has saved me . . . Where is Huaco? In my dreams, I've seen her running through the punas.

MACHULA: Huaco went to the mountains; she left with hatred in her heart. She was going to avenge your death, she said.

COYA: We have to find her, Papáy, we have to find her.

MACHULA: Yes, we have to find her . . . now that I have you, let's go look for the seeds of life. Get your quipe.[20]

COYA: Wait! What's that noise? Horses . . . are they dancing? No . . . they're running, they're running.

Coya falls to the ground in fear. Machula turns around to ritually cleanse her. Coya enters a trance.

Machula: Coya! Are you seeing your sister?

Coya: No, Papáy, Huaco is very far way . . . (*She looks around.*) It's the blue fly that announces death that I am seeing[21] . . . It wants to tell me something, it wants to announce something . . .

Machula runs to set up his mesa. He lights a candle that he hands to Coya.

Coya: It's them, Papáy, it's them! They are rising from beneath the stones, they're coming towards me, like a river runs over the earth . . .

Throughout the rest of the scene, Coya is surrounded by presences and will speak for them. Machula will assist her in the trance.

Machula: Wait, wawalláy.[22]

They both wail; Coya appears possessed by a spirit.

Machula: Let them in! What are they trying to tell you? Let them in!

Coya: It's trying to tell me something. It's trying to announce something.

Machula: Let it in!

Coya: It's trying to tell me something. It's trying to announce something. Little brother![23] What are you trying to tell me? What do you want to say?

Offstage, Andean violin music plays.

Coya (*Singing, channels the voices of the Presences*): Listen to how the trumpets sound, listen to how the drums sound. That is our blood, our life. That is our bones, our fat, our flesh.

Coya: Papáy![24] . . . Who did that to you, tell me, who did that to you?

Presence 1: Oh, they sucked out all my fat, I'm now just charqui, pure charqui.[25]

Presence 2: Tambobambino maqtatas, yawar mayu apakun.[26]

Machula: Come, daughter, I'm right here. Get up!

Presence 3: Alvergonischay . . . ![27] (*Singing*)

Coya: Yes, little brother, it's so cold here under the earth, isn't it? So cold!

Presence 1: Coya, they're the ones who stir up the evil wind to put out the fire in our hearts, to finish off the maize of life.

Presence 3: The river of blood has taken his young life, only his hat remains, and his poncho, his poncho floating there.

Coya (*Wrapped up in the presences, who are carrying her off*): Take me with you, yes! Why would I stay here? Take me with you . . .

Machula: Coya! (*He retrieves her.*) Go away! We're not ready to die yet! (*Then, to Coya*) Did you hear them? Your wandering brothers and sisters, whose souls find no rest, say the Caporal and his people are the evil wind . . . And you helped them?

Coya (*A little confused*): They tricked me! . . . I had to do it, they made me cure him . . . The Caporal was sick . . . So, they're not immortal! . . . I have to help my brothers and sisters; they've assigned me a task: to find their body parts, gather up their bones. I'll go down there, to where the sea begins, to seek justice. Maybe that way I'd have some peace, some consolation.

Machula: Surely, like the white fox you'll have to go to the coasts, immerse yourself in the seafoam. Surely, there you can find some answers about your brethren. I'll continue on my way alone.

Machula leaves. He stops. He returns to Coya and takes out his quena.[28]

Machula: Here, take my courage with you.

Coya plays the quena once; the Equeqo enters to her call. He stands behind Coya, looks out at the audience, looks at Coya, takes off his chullo and gives it to her. She looks at it, laughs, and puts it on. To thank him, she plays some music, and they dance together.

SIX
The Trial

The Judge and Scribe enter, dressed like the Machu-viejo (old man) character from the Contradanza dance in the Paucartambo Festival. They are creating a ruckus and frighten Coya. The first trial begins.

JUDGE: Showdown!

The Archangel comes forward; a dead man enters, seeking justice. They dance, and the Archangel drops his sword. The China Diabla enters, takes the sword, and re-kills the dead man. The Archangel retrieves his sword, grabs the China Diabla, lays her on the floor, and moves as if sexually violating her. He then exits. The Judge and Scribe laugh, make obscene gestures, then offer the barefoot China Diabla a pair of shoes, presumably in exchange for sex. She grabs the shoes and exits. The Judge and Scribe laugh and clown about.

JUDGE: Next case.

Coya enters and can only speak through the quena. The Judge and Scribe do not understand, and they ridicule her. They ask for the help of a translator.

Scribe: Felipe![29]

Enter Felipe.

Felipe (*Always speaking in Quechua and Spanish*): Kay warmi karu llaqtamantaraqsi hamun. Chaymantas justicia, munan. Millay wayrakunas apakun familianta manas samaytapas atinchu. This woman says she comes from afar to seek justice. The bad winds pulled her away from her family, and she can't find peace.

Coya plays her quena.

Felipe: The communities are being razed by the Caporal, who has killed many men and women. She says too that the spirits of the dead have come to her and have told her that he killed them, removing their fat. Llapan llaqtakunapis chay caporal wañuchichkan. Qariwarmikunatas. Chaymanta ninmi ayaqkuna willamunsi paymi wañuchichkan runakunata wiranta urquspa.

Coya plays her quena.

Felipe: Llapan kawsayninchik tukukapuchkanku, sarapis ñakay rikhurimun. Chayta ninmi. She says, too, that everyone's life is coming to an end, that there is almost no more maize of life. That is what she said.

SCRIBE (*Addressing the Judge in English*): In the name of the Father, the Son, and the Holy Ghost. The woman came here asking for justice. She has strange dreams with her dead parents and they told her that the man who killed them was the Caporal.[30]

JUDGE: If this woman speaks like that with the dead, what won't she talk about with the living? Does she have any family?

FELIPE (*To Coya*): Kachkanraqchu familiayki?

Coya doesn't respond.

FELIPE: Yaw, warmi, rimay, tapuchkanku. Kachkanraqchu familiayki?[31]

Coya refuses to answer. The China Diabla approaches the Scribe and mutters to him about Coya.

SCRIBE (*In English*): She has a father, and she has a dangerous sister.

JUDGE: If she doesn't want to speak, she must have something to hide. Seeresses have always been intriguing. The Holy Scriptures said so . . . Enough! She is sentenced to restless wandering, throw her out of this honorable court.

FELIPE (*To Coya*): Yaw warmi, kunanmi ripuy; pasapuy; chaynan chay; kayllanmi; justician tukukapun.[32] These

Wiracochas say that you're crazy, and they're throwing you out of courthouse. Scat!

Coya cries to Felipe with her quena for the last time.

Felipe (*To the Judge and Scribe*): Maybe this woman is right. What she's saying reminds me of stories of pishtacos I heard as a child. They say they removed the fat from people to make candles, to pay external debts, they say . . .

Judge: I can understand your reasoning and that of this woman. But, what would you do if you were in my place? What would be your arguments in her favor?

Felipe: Maybe, for the first time, these people would be heard in their own language, and I, as Judge, would understand them because I speak like them.

While he speaks, he takes the Judge's place and is vested with judicial robes.

Felipe: But . . . (*To Coya*): we'd have to see how you and yours fair against the Caporal . . . justice is blind, dear, and can't favor just you, because many would remain defenseless.

Coya (*Recovering her voice with fury, she accuses him, yelling*): What are you telling them? Are you tricking me? Look at your feet, covered with mud like mine, but the nape of your neck is like theirs, traitor, toad mouth, son of an evil mother, spawn of the devil, traitor, a thousand times traitor!

The Judge and Scribe grow furious and throw her out. Coya wraps herself in a cloth to protect herself from this nightmare. The Equeqo approaches her. The Judge, Scribe, and Felipe exit.

SEVEN
Equeqo and Coya

EQUEQO: Coya, Coya, Coya, don't sleep now.

COYA: What else can I do, if no one will listen to me?

EQUEQO: Once there was a condor who never spread his wings fully. One day his children were snatched from the nest, and the condor had to open his wings as never before, in order to recover them. That day, the condor learned how to fly against the wind. And now, . . . keep telling me your story . . .

COYA: I never thought it would be like this. Death, pure death. (*Singing*) Uñaynam kaytaqa musyarqanikuy, pimá yachanman karqa kaynatan kanantaqa, wañuyllaña puramente wañuyllaña.[33]

Equeqo exits, and Huaco appears. She's dressed for war and carries a lit torch. She feels Coya's presence.

EIGHT
The Sisters Meet

COYA: Huaco, my sister, where are you? I want to talk to you, I want to see you.

HUACO: Pim? Pim chay?[34]

COYA: You're not my sister. That face is not mine, nor that weapon, nor that fire.

HUACO: Who are you? A spirit? Go away, shoo!

COYA: No . . . it's me. I'm alive now, although for a long time I felt I was dead. Where have you been? What have you done?

HUACO: I've been wandering from town to town to join the people who are fighting. From them, I've learned to carry this fire.

COYA: So it's true that I've seen you in my dreams, up there where the bright stars grow.

HUACO: I'm taking the fire from town to town, rushing ahead, lighting immense bonfires, so the Caporal and his people stay away.

COYA: They're very strong. I've gone down to the lands where the sea begins, to search for justice, and they have people there too, some of ours too.

HUACO: Coyacha, you know: fire makes the Caporal sick.

COYA: Have you seen the other side, my sister? The earth is weeping, the cracks are splitting wider and wider, and that's where all the comuneros end up.[35] Huaco, fire will finish off everything.

HUACO: I only know that fire makes him sick and that we have to go on. Come, Coya, let's go, come with me . . . you'll be able to see for us and help us advance, arriving before us.

COYA: Why should I look into the future, if now I see our family dispersed, separated, each one out searching alone, on their own? No, Huaco, I have come to stay, to look for our tayta, now that I have found you. Let's be together! (*She sings an improvised tune*) Wayayuyay . . .

Huaco responds, setting down her vara and uncovering her face. They look at each other and sing together. They play like children. Huaco falls.

HUACO: I'm tired, ñañáy.

COYA: Let's rest, even if just for a moment.

HUACO: I can't sleep, I can't sleep. I have to be alert, on the highest point on the mountain, watching to see if the evil winds appear . . .

COYA: And I always have to close my eyes to be able to look inside. Sometimes, I can't open them again, and I feel like I'm dead. Something is going to happen, I know it, I feel it, the evil wind is advancing, the Caporal and his people will bring it.

HUACO: We'll finish them off with fire, and then everything will be different, better! And then we three can be together again.

Sisters Huaco (left) and Coya. Photograph by Miguel Villafañe.

Coya: How much longer can the bonfires keep growing? And when you have nothing more to burn, you will light human torches!

Huaco: We'll kill them first. Remember how we were before. Now, we defend ourselves and they retreat.

Trumpets sound.

Coya: Our time is growing short. Wait here! Let's look for the Auqui.[36]

Huaco: No, come with me. We have to continue!

Coya: I have to stay here. If not, the fire will burn us both.

Huaco: Look . . . a dust storm is forming. I have to move on. Hamuy! Hamuy![37] (*She disappears.*)

Coya begins to dream, or perhaps she awakens from her dream.

Coya: Huaco . . . dear sister . . . I've seen it in my dreams . . . It's not just fire . . . we have to go . . . Huaco! Don't leave . . . Let's go look for my tayta . . . Papáy! Papáy!

NINE
The Contradanza

Coya is in the Community.[38] *The Archangel and China appear; both drunk, they harass each other. The Archangel arrives at the house, slices the air with his sword, falls upon Coya, and tries to rape her. Jealous, China pulls him away, and Coya, terrified, rejects him. The Archangel and China become furious; they make the earth tremble, and beat her with winds.*

Coya: What do you want now? Didn't I cure your boss? Didn't I cure your Caporal already? Huh? Is it my fault he's still sick?

The Archangel and China beat her with winds, like whips.

Coya: All right, all right, fine, yes . . . I had a dream. Tell him, I dreamt that people were chasing him with large mule prods that they hung from his ear . . . and with urine filled with spicy pepper that they threw at him, and he ran off . . . afraid! (*She bursts into laughter, making fun of them.*)

The Archangel and China are furious. China finds Machula's hat and mimics his singing, while the Archangel threatens to crush it.

Coya: No! Fine, I will tell you what weakens your Caporal . . . (*She pulls fire out of her sleeves and begins to throw it*). It's fire that is killing him! Fire!

They run off frightened. Coya recovers the hat.

TEN
The Nightmare

The Equeqo enters. Coya gives him Machula's hat.

Coya: I wanted to see him again! (*She enters into a trance.*) I shut my eyes again to look inside better, and to see if there I could find them, Huaco, my siblings, my Tayta, but now everything is different. There were new apparitions, and everything was whirling about me . . . The embers are crackling . . . Will I cry or will I sing? Am I asleep or awake? I hear my Tayta's vara coming down the hills, and Huaco's steps coming from the other side. But they don't know it; they don't hear each other.

In the fog of her trance, Huaco and Machula appear. The three begin a quiet dance, coming together and separating.

ELEVEN
The Planting

The three arrive.

HUACO: I have seen the Archangel entering towns with sword in hand. Someone told him about the fire!

COYA: It was me.

HUACO: Iskay uya! Two-faced hypocrite!

COYA: I had to tell him so my father could escape. (*At the moment, Machula presents a small sack with the seeds of life.*) You've gathered the seeds in the midst of such horror! You've kept your word. Seeds of life that grow in the alluvium, in the purest snow, even in death itself . . . the seed of life . . .

HUACO: The towns were advancing with fire in hand. The Caporal was retreating. We have been able to beat him.

COYA: You're fooling yourself. Fire makes him sick, but doesn't kill him.

HUACO: Why did you have to tell him?

COYA: I had to tell him because we needed time . . . to find each other again.

HUACO (*Attacking*): Time for what? Now that the Caporal is advancing, there's no more time!

COYA: Listen to me! Now that the three of us are together, this is the time to plant the seeds of life. That will be the end of the Caporal and his people.

MACHULA (*Taking out the fetuses*[39]): There they are, the black fox and the white fox, they're circling, bringing death.

HUACO: We haven't gone out to bring death!

MACHULA: So much time on different paths, to meet up again with hatred in our hearts; I've travelled so far searching for both of you. You, running up towards the mountains like the black fox, and you, like the white fox, running down towards the coast to dive into the seafoam. All that just to hear, to hear death and rancor in your mouths, your hearts. That does nothing for my hope.

Coya and Huaco stop fighting.

HUACO: Papáy, you gave me strength to go out and fight.

COYA: You gave me courage to keep seeking justice.

MACHULA: I forged my path by going up and down the mountains, by walking beside the rivers, and I found the seeds of life . . . But it doesn't matter, it's too late . . . I sense the blue fly that announces death . . . buzzing in my ears.

Coya: Papáy, don't die. You're the Auqui, and now we're together again. Wifala Taytáy.[40]

Huaco cheers. Coya takes their father's vara, picks it up, and cleans it. Huaco strikes her vara with seeds and returns it to Machula. The three are now together. Coya and Huaco finally sow the seeds of life while the Auqui (Machula) dances and sings. The three plant seeds. The Archangel appears with his sword lit up. China appears, as does the Caporal carrying a lit Catherine wheel, and they destroy everything. The father and two daughters are buried under the hills. The Archangel, China, and Caporal disappear. Coya comes out from under the hill, gives the maize of life to the Equeqo, and goes back under the hill.

Equeqo (*While planting*): This maize was given to me by this woman who, coming out from the hills, told me this story and gave me this task. So that someday the sun and the moon may join together, the bull and the Amaru[41] see each other, the world move forward, the earth tremble, the dusk dawn, and the reptiles become fireflies, illuminating everything.

Music. The Equeqo dances among the hills.

END

Notes

1. In general terms, the Andean world is divided into *hanaq pacha*, which is the upper world, the heavens and celestial beings, and the realm of the gods; *kay pacha*, which is the perceptible, physical world that human beings inhabit; and *ukhu* (or *hurin*) *pacha*, which is the underworld or the inner earth.

2. *Hanaq Pachap Kusikuynin* translates to "joy of heaven." This Quechua hymn to the Virgin Mary was published in 1631 by the Franciscan friar Juan Pérez Bocanegra, who claimed authorship; the first two verses are reproduced here. Both musically and poetically, the song is an example of Christian-Quechua syncretism.

3. "Joy of heaven / a thousand times adored / blessed fruit / hope of all humanity / sustainer of the weak / hear my prayer / Hear our prayers / Oh ivory column, mother of God / Magnificent iris, yellow and white / receive this hymn we offer you / come to our aid / reveal to us the fruit of your womb."

4. In Andean culture, the Equeqo is a demigod or spirit of good fortune and prosperity. Traditionally, he is presented as a short, stout, mustached man wearing a *chullo* ("knit wool hat") and poncho, and carrying various objects: money, food, household objects, and other items representing prosperity.

5. The *-y* suffix denotes the possessive "my." In this case, the term borrows from the Spanish *papá* ("father") and adds the Quechua suffix to mean "my father."

6. The original dialogue sometimes immediately repeats in Quechua what has just been said in Spanish, or vice versa, as in this case—*Yachaq* means *sabio*, or wise man. When that happens, no additional translation of the Quechua is provided, unless absolutely necessary for clarity.

7. *Puna*—Andean tundra.

8. This story comes from one of several Andean myths that revolve around two foxes, one from "above" (the Andean highlands) and one from "below" (the coast). The foxes represent two poles or opposing forces that must be brought into balance, or harmony, reflected by the characters of the two sisters in the play. This particular version is that of the "Devouring Foxes," collected and translated from the original Quechua by the anthropologist Alejandro Ortiz Rescaniere (see Ortiz Rescaniere, "Los zorros devoradores," *Revista de la Universidad Católica*, no. 2, 31 Dec. 1977, pp. 85–93). My appreciation to Carlos Molina-Vital for the reference for this source.

9. *Vara*—Staff, traditionally carried by male Indigenous community leaders.

10. "Enough! Thieves, evil winds, go away! Even with the rain you can't beat us!"

11. "Father, that awful wind is taking my sister! Now we're all alone, crying. Why did we wait until now?"

12. *Wayra*—wind.

13. *Mesa*—An altar spread out on the ground by a healer to perform healing rituals. In this scene, Coya lays her *q'ipirina* ("queperina" in Andean Spanish)—a woolen cloth used by women in daily life to carry bundles on their backs—on the floor to place the objects she will use. Generally, ritual healing objects might include coca leaves and other herbs, food, alcohol, stick brushes, stones, shells, knives, statues of saints, rosaries, cigarettes, coins, etc., each with its own symbolic value.

14. *Tayta*—Father in Quechua.

15. "Coya, dear Coya, my dear Coya! Where are you? Where have you disappeared to, my sister?"

16. *Ñañáy*—my sister.

17. *Apus*—Sacred mountains that are living spirits.

18. "Because of you I come again / Just like long ago / Seeking your help for us / At the night's end / So I bring this most beautiful flower / Place it on my head / So my eyes can see clearly."

19. "So, this is where you've been, my child."

20. *Quipe*—Andean Spanish term for "bundle," from the Quechua *qipi* or *q'ipi*.

21. Quechua people believe that the *chiririnka*, a dark blue fly, foretells death. For a detailed exploration of the *chiririnka* in relation to experiences and interpretations of death and dying during the Internal Armed Conflict and regarding postwar exhumations of mass graves, see Isaías Rojas-Pérez, *Mourning Remains: State Atrocity, Exhumations, and Governing the Disappeared in Peru's Postwar Andes*, Stanford UP, 2017, especially pp. 165–171.

22. "My child."

23. Here, "little brother" is a term of endearment used to address another person, not a literal sibling.

24. In this case, Coya is using "Papáy" as an honorific to refer to one of the presences speaking to her, not to her father.

25. *Charqui*—Dried meat.

26. "They say the river of blood is taking away the young men of Tambobamba." *Tambobambino maqta* is a reference to a popular carnival

song from Tambobamba, in the Apurímac region, which Arguedas described as the cruelest and most beautiful song he had ever heard (119). In the song, the evidence of the young man's life left floating are the musical instruments he had played, rather than his clothes as depicted here (José María Arguedas, "El Carnaval de Tambobamba," *Indios, mestizos y señores*, 3rd ed., Editorial Horizonte, 1989, pp. 117–20). In the play, the "river of blood" is also a reference to the Internal Armed Conflict. The leader of Shining Path, Abimael Guzmán, advocated violence and proclaimed to his followers that the movement would have to cross through a "river of blood" for their revolution to succeed.

27. *Alvergonischay*—The title of a traditional *huayno* ("a popular Andean music and dance genre") that employs an allegory of how *alverjas* ("sweet peas") are cultivated, dried, and used as food to talk about the fate of orphans. ("Alvergonischa," *LUM Centro de Documentación e Investigación*, lum.cultura.pe/cdi/audio/alvergonischa, accessed 29 Jan. 2025). My appreciation to Carlos Molina-Vital for this reference.

28. *Quena*—A traditional Andean flute made of reeds or wood, consisting of one long tube with six holes and one thumb hole.

29. The name of the translator, Felipe, recalls Felipillo, the Indigenous translator for the Spaniards during the conquest of Peru. Interpreting in the sixteenth century between the conqueror Francisco Pizarro, the friar Vicente de Valverde, and the Incan Emperor Atahuallpa, Felipillo relayed the Spaniards' demands that Indigenous peoples accept Spanish rule and convert to Christianity. Atahuallpa's refusal led to his imprisonment and execution by the Spaniards. Because of his role as intermediary during the conquest, Felipillo's name is synonymous with traitor in the Andean world.

30. While not entirely grammatically correct (to dream *with* rather than *about* betrays Spanish lexico-grammatical influence), by speaking in English, the Scribe is likely trying to position himself as superior to his interlocutors.

31. "Hey, woman, answer, they are asking you a question. Is your family still alive?"

32. "Hey, woman, get out, go on! That's it, that's all, this trial has concluded."

33. "A long time ago, we predicted this. Who by chance would have known that it will be this way? Just death, purely and solely death."

34. "Who, who's there?"

35. *Comuneros*—members of *ayllus*, independent Indigenous communities.

36. *Auqui (Awki)*—A term that in Quechua of the Southern Andes means "prince" and "grandfather," invoking nobility or higher rank. In this case Coya is referring to Machula.

37. "Come! Come!"

38. The "Community" is the *ayllu*, the Indigenous community that is a basic unit of Andean social structure. In the play, Coya sits on a large rectangular cloth meant to indicate her house.

39. Alpaca and llama fetuses are used in rituals of thanksgiving and adoration of Pachamama, Mother Earth.

40. *Wifala*—Hooray!

41. The bull and the Amaru ("serpent," also referring to a double-headed serpent deity) represent Spanish and Andean cultures, respectively.

Goodbye Ayacucho (1990)

In *Goodbye Ayacucho* (based on a homonymous novella by Julio Ortega), Augusto Casafranca portrays Alfonso Cánepa, a peasant leader who was disappeared, tortured, and murdered by state authorities. In the play, Cánepa is unable to enter the next life because his killer took some of his bones as souvenirs—in Andean culture the body must be intact for the spirit to rest. The opening scene reveals Cánepa's clothes laid out in a traditional Andean act of mourning. In a corner, a woman in a black pollera sits on a blanket, surrounded by various traditional Andean instruments. Q'olla, a dancer from the Andean Qhapaq Qolla *comparsa* ("carnival procession group"), also played by Casafranca, comes across the clothing, and then steals and puts on the shoes, giving Cánepa's spirit the opportunity to take over Q'olla's voice. The reembodiment of Cánepa's spirit in Q'olla is culturally significant: the latter's costume is that of a recognizable figure—the Qhapaq Q'olla—from the Virgin of Carmen Festival in Paurcartambo, in the province of Cuzco.[1] The actor remains dressed as a Qhapaq Q'olla, with the figure's typical white woolen mask covering his face for the majority of the play; only at the end does he appear dressed fully as Cánepa, after donning the suit that had been laid out at the beginning. Throughout the play, the shifts in character between Cánepa and Q'olla are primarily indicated through dialogue content and intonation—the actor adopts a typical falsetto when Q'olla speaks.

Casafranca has a collection of woolen Q'olla masks, each with a slightly different expression, from which he chooses before each performance. For Casafranca, the fact that a unique version of the Qhapaq Q'olla appears in each iteration "refuerza la naturaleza colectiva del personaje" ("reinforces the collective nature of the character"). During the festivals, the Qhapaq Q'olla *comparsas* are composed of many individuals, each with their own life story, who come together for a common ritual, celebratory purpose. Before each performance of *Goodbye Ayacucho*, Casafranca wonders, "¿Quién va a salir esta noche?" ("Who is going to come out tonight?") (Casafranca).

A video of a performance of the play is available in the online digital library of the Hemispheric Institute (Grupo Cultural Yuyachkani).

Note

1. *Q'olla*—a dancer from the mestizo Qhapaq Qolla *comparsas* in Paucartambo, Cuzco. As a Q'olla, this dancer represents a poor llama herder from the Q'ollao plateau. See Zoila S. Mendoza, *Shaping Society Through Dance: Mestizo Ritual Performance in the Peruvian Andes*. U of Chicago P, 2000.

Works Cited

Casafranca, Augusto. Interview. Conducted by Anne Lambright, 4 Aug. 2023.

Grupo Cultural Yuyachkani. *Adiós Ayacucho*. Directed by Miguel Rubio Zapata, 1990. *Hemispheric Institute*, hemisphericinstitute.org/en/hidvl-collections/item/75-yuyachkani-adios-ayacucho.html.

Character List

In order of appearance:

WOMAN

ALFONSO CÁNEPA

Q'OLLA

On the stage there is a platform on which the clothes of a disappeared man (jacket, pants, shoes) are displayed, as if for a wake. At the foot of the platform, flowers and candles. In the far right corner of the stage, on a blanket, a woman surrounded by instruments provides musical accompaniments. To the far left, there is a large black plastic bag, in which Q'olla is hiding.

Q'olla emerges from a black plastic bag. Photograph by Miguel Rubio Zapata.

Q'OLLA (*Emerging from the large black bag*[1] *with a small white flag in hand, discovers the vigil and approaches it.*): Yaw, pitaq kay runari, kakalláw, wañukapusqachusina ay urpicha, sunqucha imaraykuchá eh? Llapan llaqtakunapi askha qhari-warmikuna wañukapushanku, chinkapushanku. Ay wayqicháy . . . Mira wayqilláy.[2]

Looking at the dead man's shoes.

That's of no use to you anymore, and I need them . . . Excuse me . . .

He stands up on the shoes and begins to quake.

ALFONSO CÁNEPA: I came to Lima . . .

Q'OLLA: . . . to recover my cadaver . . .

ALFONSO CÁNEPA: That's how my speech would begin . . .

Q'OLLA: . . . once I got in the city.

This isn't my voice. Pin kanki. Who are you?[3]

Imatan munanki, maypin kashanki.[4]

ALFONSO CÁNEPA: That's what I was thinking as I crawled out of the pit where they had tossed me, after burning and mutilating me, leaving me for dead, and missing half of my bones, which they took to Lima.

In Quinua,[5] last week, during this month of July, a dry month, I decided to appear in person at the police station. On seeing me enter, the sergeant stood up.

"Don't play dumb. You're a dangerous terrorist." I knew they'd accuse me of being a terrorist, and they knew that I wasn't. What did they want me to confess?

Q'OLLA: What a mess you got yourself into, brother . . .

ALFONSO CÁNEPA: First, they ripped off part of my pinky, and I didn't even notice. I only saw the blood when they tore off part of another finger. I screamed so much. At that moment I must have understood that they weren't going to hold back, and now my body wouldn't stop shaking. Afterwards they took me out to the edge of town, next to the big hill and close to the ravine. There, they hurled me from a moving jeep. I fell, tumbled down screaming, reaching for a rock, a ditch where I could hide.

Q'OLLA: And?

ALFONSO CÁNEPA: But, they threw a grenade at me that exploded very close by, and I could see, as if I were someone else, how my right arm flew off, waving goodbye to me through the air. I fell, knowing I would die.

Q'OLLA: Well there, you could have tried to hide anywhere you could, brother.

ALFONSO CÁNEPA: Another phosphorus grenade blew up at my back, emptying my skull and splitting my stomach as if it were made of rags.

While I was flying through the air, I saw those soldiers running down the hillside, howling like wolves. Someone picked me up by my right foot. Then I realized I was missing my left leg. They were dragging me to the bottom of that hill, where the rocks are bigger and the grass sharper, but they dragged me so poorly that I lost other bones along the way. From then on, I would have to keep precise account of my lost parts, so I could find them again later and give myself a proper burial.

But when they finally tossed me into a wide, shallow hole, and began to cover me with rocks and wild grass, I thought I saw one of those policemen digging around, with a plastic bag in hand, and immediately knew that that son of a bitch was gathering my parts to take half my body with him.

This same policeman, before throwing me into the hole that would be my tomb, filled my belly with stones and straw as if I were a doll assembled to be disassembled.

I lay there dying for a long time, or maybe I was already dead, when they covered me with rocks and weeds, and I entertained myself thinking about my own condition as a gullible Peruvian.

Q'OLLA: Of course, only a fool would go to the police station knowing they were after him.

Alfonso Cánepa: I lay there remembering and became enraged. This time, the fury was for myself. Everyone knew they were killing everywhere, and that some of those detained turned up a month later in mass graves, their bodies tortured. But they had torn me apart. Missing an arm and a leg, I couldn't go very far, for that very reason, because I only have half a body.

I began to slither, to sneak off, to roll a bit until I finally pulled myself up next to a fallen, burned tree I found along the way. I started to climb that hill slowly, and once on top I saw the town below, dark and red. I felt a great, calm sadness and screamed. Or rather, what came out was an ugly rumbling, like that of a wet cat. I cried out once again, "Give me back my body! Where have you taken my bones?"

No matter what, I will go to Lima to recover what is mine.

Q'olla: Yaw ripunaymi kashan.[6] I have things to do, too. Ruwanaymi wayqicháy.[7] Look, I wish you the best of luck. May things go well for you. Tupananchiskama wayqicháy.[8]

The woman plays a musical accompaniment. Q'olla senses that Cánepa's shoes are speaking to him, and he feels a vague threat. He approaches and moves away from the shoes several times, but eventually puts them on.

Q'olla senses that Cánepa's shoes are speaking to him. Photograph by Miguel Rubio Zapata.

Alfonso Cánepa: Dawn was breaking when I sat down to wait for don Luciano's cart to go by; he's the old man who distributes milk in the town every day. As soon as I saw him, I jumped up on the back of the cart, like the kids do when they're playing, only I did it so he wouldn't see me. Don Luciano was wrapped up in his scarf, which was older than his tan mule, and if the poor man saw me, he would cry.

He begins to skip in place on the platform, imitating the sound of the cart travelling over the cobbled streets.

The cart entered the town through the first cobbled street and, as always, stopped at the first house, where the Robles live. Immediately, the door opened and Rosa Robles stepped out, greeting us. I, too, responded to her greeting, and if she heard it, she must have thought it some whim of the decrepit mule.

"Oh, don Luciano, what have you heard about Alfonsito?"

"What do you think? Word is they killed him."

"They're coming from Lima, people say they're killing everywhere."

"There's nothing to be done anymore; everything's wiped out when the government kills."

The cart moved on, this time turning onto a packed dirt road. I tried to sit up to see the streets of my childhood for the last time, but I stopped myself.

"They've killed him. His soul will not find rest; we need to find his body. He must be given a Christian burial," said my mother.

"If you hear anything, don Luciano, come tell us," said my father.

To me, his voice sounded far and distant. Or maybe because I had lost half my body I could only hear half of what my parents say. Or maybe I lost the half that came from him, and that's why I hear his voice that way.

"Papa, mama, so much death! So much suffering!

"Scat, dog, scat!" cried don Luciano.

From Ayacucho to Lima took four days. So far, no one had discovered me and with luck no one would. Upon arriving to Lima, I might have to reveal myself. People there are used to seeing dead bodies on television. Once I told them my story, there would be no lack of volunteers to bury me. "Wait for me, Mr. President, I want to see you!" I cried out suddenly. But this time the dogs started barking like crazy. The milk from the jugs had splattered all over me, and, on top of that, the straw from the cart had stuck all over my body. I must have looked like one of those dolls from the highlands that can withstand both the cold and the snow.[9]

To musical accompaniment, he jumps off the platform as if descending from the cart and begins to walk about, searching for a truck that could take him to Lima.

In the congested loading station, I found a truck: "El Peruanito," *the little Peruvian*, though the name gave me a bit of pause.

Q'olla: Sure, it could have fallen off a cliff and killed you twice for your doubly countryman condition.

Alfonso Cánepa: But it was the best truck, full of boxes of fruit and sacks of potatoes. So I dragged myself through the cargo until I nestled in a corner near the cabin. Meanwhile the driver and his helper poured themselves some early morning nips to fight off the cold. Finally, they casually started the motor and turned on the radio.

We were moving along slowly, when I discovered that someone was whistling next to me. I couldn't contain my fright. Startled, I uncovered myself and saw how the face of the whistling man stopped whistling, and his eyes grew wider and wider. He stared at me as if this were normal. Suddenly, the truck veered off the road on a narrow curve. It passed through a treelined path and paused in front of a small cemetery. I felt an irresistible panic. The truck stopped. The driver climbed up to remove some sacks and uncovered my face.

Q'olla: He must not have recognized you either.

Alfonso Cánepa: I still have my doubts, because he immediately pulled out a black plastic bag.

Q'olla: That must have been left over from some burial.

Alfonso Cánepa: Meanwhile, the helper was coming back, after leaving a bouquet of flowers on some tomb. We were returning to the main road, a very bad road, by the way. With hundreds of potholes and thousands of curves. All the clattering about was grinding my bones.

Q'olla: The few you had left, anyway.

Alfonso Cánepa: It must have been after leaving Abancay,[10] more or less, that I began to notice the people who were crossing the roadway every so often. Others were sitting on enormous stones. The suspicion that they were, like me, disappeared, terrified me. Was it possible I was not the only one going to Lima to recover his bones? When suddenly . . .

"Silence . . . looks like a military patrol."

"What branch do you think?"

"Is that a jeep or a truck?"

"Truck," someone else said. "And they could be sinchis."[11]

"No, here the sinchis only travel by air."

Humph, it turned out to be an army truck.

"What's going on? Why are you stopped?" asked the pale young lieutenant.

"Nothing, lieutenant," replied the driver. "Just checking the battery, but we're leaving now."

"And that?" he asked, pointing to me.

I kept still. My arm was falling to one side and my leg to another. False alarm, they didn't recognize me either. Then, they stepped back, and I pulled myself together as best I could.

We hadn't gone much further, when an unfamiliar noise halted us. Suddenly, coming at us from the other side, was a military patrol full of marines, in a truck that was a veritable fortress.[12]

We saw they were escorting ten young prisoners who were singing a dark litany in Ayacucho Quechua. I saw their full faces, their simple eyes, their cheeks burned by the cold, their coarse hair. There was no mystery about them; they were made of flesh and bones like anyone else. Only they were somewhat more so because they knew they would be killed, and that fact produced in them the madness of those final moments. So much death, so much desperation, and it's like nothing. The truck stopped right by ours.

The marines looked at each other calmly. The young captives clinched their fists silently.

"Bye, and be careful on this road," said the captain.

And then they drove on. We immediately took off, too.

During the following monologue, night falls. Cánepa/Q'olla takes one of the candles. He remembers he is surrounded by cadavers, and he approaches the platform.

Soon we would arrive in Huanta, another of the bases of the military's counterinsurgency efforts.[13] Not long before, secret tombs, enormous mass graves, had been discovered there. The cadavers were still in the plaza, unrecognizable. While the mothers howled in chorus, searching for their dead, I heard the cracking of their bones, their intermittent weeping. So much death! So much desperation! And so little . . . !

Using the candle, Cánepa/Q'olla lights some firecrackers behind the platform. As they go off, there is a festive atmosphere. Cánepa/Q'olla marches about as if in a military procession, with soldiers and music.

At the entrance to the town, we were delayed by a group of people in a state of total frenzy, circling a half-naked preacher who was announcing the end of the world. When we got to the plaza, we saw a funeral procession entering and heading towards the main church, where the authorities were waiting in the atrium. They must have executed some local boss, I thought. A funeral trumpet called for silence and as soon as there was quiet, in the distance we could hear dynamite explosions that made the earth tremble. Immediately, the plaza filled with soldiers. We moved forward blasting the horn, braking and accelerating. At the town's edge, this time in an elegant neighborhood, we saw another group of better dressed people who listened to their own windbag promising them the peace that would come with the world's end.

Q'olla takes the colorful collection of tassels from his waist and begins to narrate the following letter, touching each string as if reading a khipu.[14]

Q'OLLA: This is the first letter I imagined.

Mr. President:

Herewith, I, the undersigned, Alfonso Cánepa, Peruvian citizen, resident of Quinua, farmer by occupation, communicate the following to you, as the maximum political authority of the Republic:

On the 15th of July, I was arrested by my town's civil guard, taken away, held incommunicado, tortured, burned, mutilated, killed. They declared me disappeared.[15]

You must have seen the national protest that has arisen in my name; I now add my own protest, requesting that you return the portion of my bones that was taken to Lima. As you well know, all of the nation's laws and all of the international treaties, as well as all of the Human Rights charters, proclaim not only the inalienable right to human life, but also to a proper death with a proper burial of the whole body. The fundamental duty to respect human life presupposes another, even more fundamental one, which is a wartime code of honor: the dead, sir, may not be mutilated. The cadaver is, shall we say, the most basic unit of death, and to divide it, as is done today in Peru, is to shatter both natural and social law. Your anthropologists and intellectuals have determined that violence originates in the System and in the State that you represent. One of your victims who has nothing left to lose is telling you this. I'm telling you this from my own experience. I want my bones, I want my literal, entire body, even if it is entirely dead.

In the end, I seriously doubt you will read what I have written. An ancestor more candid than I am wrote a letter over two thousand pages long to the King of Spain that was not read until more than two hundred years had passed.[16] On the other hand, Valverde's speech, or the Uchuraccay speech, are likely read in all the nation's schools, like two pillars of the State.[17]

In closing, I hope you will do everything possible to delay my burial no longer.

Q'olla returns to Cánepa's suit, picks up the pants, and begins to put them on.

Oh, wayqichalláy,[18] thank you, dear brother. I think these will fit me very well, and besides I'm going to need them to keep on travelling.

Q'olla begins to put on Cánepa's jacket as Cánepa speaks.

Alfonso Cánepa: The truck climbed through a long chain of mountains, over deep abysses. Slowly. Then all of a sudden, as we passed over a narrow bridge, an explosion threw up a whirlwind of rubble and dirt. A group of armed youth surrounded us.

"Nobody move," one of them ordered, aiming his weapon at us.

Immediately, they began to unload part of the cargo we were carrying, taking it to a small, dilapidated truck that was backing up through a cloud of dust. Our driver decided to ask for a receipt, to be able to prove later that they had confiscated the cargo, and that produced a violent argument with the chief of the operation, who turned out to be a woman, who threatened to shoot him on the spot. (And there was no reason to doubt her intention). Passing by my side, she said to me:

"You see? That's what you get for being a reformer. You're neither dead nor alive. Do you want to come with us?"

"No. Thank you very much."

"Except for power, everything is an illusion. Give this man a receipt right away."

She signed and handed the receipt to the driver, who had not stopped sweating. Then, they quickly departed in another cloud of dust. We, too, were left tired and quiet. The driver shared the coffee in his thermos, and some corn bread was passed around.

The woman begins to play a melody and Q'olla adds lyrics.

Ñasya killapas ripukuchkanña
Ñasya intipas altunchikpiña
Hakuchik niñachay, haku Huamangata
Taytamamayki, qammanta waqachkan . . .[19]

While singing "Huérfano pajarillo" (Little Orphan Bird), a traditional huayno from Ayacucho, Cánepa slowly removes the Q'olla costume, dons his own jacket, and appears for the first time fully as Cánepa on stage.

When we arrived at the gates of the big city, we came upon different businesses in the waystation: food stands, shysters, bribe-takers, photographers, police. The families of the disappeared searched through each other's photos of dead loved ones. It looked like a card game in which they were shuffling their children's fates. The avenue was filled with cars. Whenever a red light stopped traffic, an enormous crowd of all types of beggars and children appeared, circulating among the cars with an anguished clamor. As soon as I entered the first street, I recognized an intense, and familiar, odor: Lima smelled distinctly of urine.

When I passed through a throng of sellers and buyers, I was overcome upon seeing there was a third crowd made up of all types of crazies and lunatics, hurriedly running to and fro. They were talking to themselves, dressed in rags or naked or grimy. Finally, I had a practical idea. I would pass myself off as a madman and that way no one would notice me. I couldn't believe it: a peddler woman offered me an orange. Another gave me a little consoling pat. Others looked at me with a kindness that frightened me, at first.

The cathedral was almost empty at that moment. From the bell tower one could see the expansive Plaza de Armas main square below, the Presidential Palace, and assault guards surrounding every corner. Little by little, all kinds of beggars, and one-armed people, limping people, crippled people, so many sick people began arriving that I decided to come down. I would pass myself off as a beggar.

"Excuse me. Can you tell me why we are here?"

"The President is going to give a speech on the need for Christian charity."

What luck! I can deliver my letter in person! Commands were shouted at the palace doors. Finally, the President, in person, with his arm raised, positioned himself in the middle of his escorts and began to walk forward until he stopped directly in front of me. I couldn't believe it. There was the man responsible for my death, but certainly he didn't even know my name, and he'd have more than one excuse to prove his personal innocence. He was clearly a politician. But, if the laws mean anything, he was directly responsible for the country's multiplying deaths, even if there were no formal sanctions. Now that his term was ending, at the very least he should feel the gaze of one of his victims. To me, his voice sounded kind but remote. I don't know whom he was addressing, but certainly not us. We would remember him, nevertheless, not for the number of votes, but for the number of dead.

I got as close as I could to him and extended my letter, and saw him place it in the pocket of his blue blazer. A blow from a rifle butt sent me flying through the air and tumbling at his feet. His bodyguard searched me from head to toe; I couldn't believe it . . .

A young boy with surprising courage rescued me.

"Stop, stop, that's my father!" he yelled.

And the taciturn guards immediately let me go.

I was putting myself together, helped by this child, when on the dark ground I saw my letter, crumpled and unopened. I felt again alone and unsure of what to do. I looked at the closed balconies of the City Hall, the Presidential Palace, where the Conquistador Francisco Pizarro had been assassinated. I looked at the vast Plaza de Armas, now almost empty.

"Come on, let's go, I'll hide you in the caves of the Rímac river," the boy said.

We were about to turn the corner at the Palace when, upon seeing the Cathedral, I hesitated . . .

"Hey, wait, come with me."

Cánepa takes the strip of candles from the front of the platform and steps up on it. The woman plays church organ-like music on an accordion.

The darkness under the great vaults was now even greater. As we passed the tomb of Francisco Pizarro I stopped, hesitant. It was a glass and marble casket, the golden Spanish lion on top, and the remains of the fierce founder of Lima could be seen: a consumed skull and a few loose bones.

Cánepa places the candles back on the ground.

"Listen, come, help me. We have to remove this heavy lid. Take this, Pizarro's actual skull. You can sell it. And these bones, too, except these, which I need."

The boy looked me in the eyes and said, "Hey, everyone will think you are Pizarro. That's okay, we'll bring you flowers. But I promise that when I'm president I will find your bones," he swore solemnly.

Cánepa moves his arms as if to hug the boy, thank him, and say goodbye. He picks the candles up again. The final words are filtered through sound effects so that his voice sounds distant, as if coming from beyond the grave.

My voice sounded like another in the ample tomb. I heard myself in the echo and understood that my hour was near. Soon I would rise from this earth, like a column of stone and fire.

He begins to blow out each candle, one by one, keeping time with the notes the woman plays on a zampoña,[20] *until everything goes black.*

END

Notes

1. The large black plastic bag is meant to evoke the bags sometimes used to store or haul corpses of victims of the Internal Armed Conflict. Presumably, before the start of the action, Q'olla had found and hidden in one to escape an unidentified pursuer.

2. "Oh, who is that man? What a shame! He looks dead. Oh, dear, oh little dove, why did he die? In all of the towns, so many men and women are dying, and disappearing. Oh, my brother, look." While the story takes place in the Ayacucho region, where a variety of Quechua known as Chanka is spoken, Q'olla, as a character from Paucartambo, speaks the Cuzco variety of Southern Quechua.

3. In the original, sometimes the dialogue immediately repeats in Spanish what has been said in Quechua. When that happens, no additional translation of the Quechua is provided.

4. "What do you want? Where are you?"

5. Quinua—a small town in the Province of Huamanga, Department of Ayacucho.

6. "Hey, I have to go."

7. "I have things to do, brother."

8. "Until we meet again, brother."

9. A reference to the dolls (*luichitos* or *guaguas*) carried by *ukukos* during the Q'oyllur Rit'i festival in Cuzco. The *ukuko* carries in one hand a doll reproduction of himself, called an *almita* (little soul). This refer-

ence reinforces a central motif in the play, where each character talks to his "other self."

10. Abancay—the capitol city of the Apurímac region of southern-central Peru.

11. *Sinchis*—A specialized police unit primarily dedicated to counterinsurgency and anti-drug trafficking. They played a central role in the government response to Shining Path and were found to have committed gross human rights violations during the Internal Armed Conflict.

12. The marines were in charge of the counterinsurgency forces in Ayacucho during the state of emergency declared by the government in the 1980s. They were responsible for the death and disappearance of tens of thousands of Andean Indigenous people.

13. *Huanta*— one of the provinces in Ayacucho most affected by Shining Path terrorism and the military's violent counterinsurgency response.

14. *Khipu*—a recording or accounting device used by many preconquest Andean cultures. *Khipus* consisted of thick, colorful, knotted threads that encoded information that could be read by specialists, the *khipu kamayuq*.

15. City police forces in charge of crime prevention and keeping the peace, the Civil Guard was an independent institution under the Secretary of the Interior that has since been absorbed into the Peruvian National Police.

16. Cánepa refers here to Felipe Guaman Poma de Ayala, a Quechua nobleman who authored a seventeenth-century letter to King Phillip III of Spain, *El primer nueva corónica y buen gobierno* (*The First New Chronicle and Good Government*), denouncing the harsh mistreatment of Indigenous peoples by Spanish colonizers. Sent in 1615, the letter was not widely read until its discovery in the Danish Royal Library in 1908. The gap is almost three hundred years, not two hundred as stated in the play. See Felipe Guaman Poma de Ayala, *Nueva crónica y buen gobierno*, edited by John V. Murra et al., Siglo XXI, 1987, 3 vols.

17. Cánepa refers here to the infamous "requerimiento," that Fray Vicente de Valverde read to Atahuallpa in 1532, demanding that the Incan convert to Catholicism and recognize the Spanish Crown. He also refers to the 1983 Uchuraccay Commission Report, principally authored by Mario Vargas Llosa, which found three Indigenous *comuneros* (members of independent Indigenous communities) guilty of killing eight

journalists during the Shining Path conflict, a finding many scholars have questioned, and which portrayed Indigenous peoples as archaic and innately prone to violence.

18. "My dear brother."

19. "Now, that the moon itself is hiding / Now, that the sun itself is up high / come, little girl, let's go to Huamanga / your father and mother are sad without you."

20. *Zampoña*—a traditional Andean pan flute.

Antígona (2000)

Antígona is a one-woman version of Sophocles's classic tragedy, performed by one of Yuyachkani's founding members, Teresa Ralli, with a collaboratively created script by the Peruvian poet José Watanabe. In this adaptation of the Greek drama, Ralli performs all roles: a female narrator; the newly crowned Creonte; Antígona herself; Hemón (Creonte's son and Antígona's love); a royal guard; and the blind prophet Tiresias. Role changes are indicated through variations in the actress's voice and gestures, such as a loud clap, how she drapes a long cape, and, at times, adjustments to the stage lighting and sound. The only props on stage are one wooden chair and a box containing the death mask of Polinices, Antígona's dead, unburied brother.

At first glance, the play seems to be a departure from Yuyachkani's other work exploring recognizably Peruvian issues: peasant uprisings in the highlands, internal migration from the highlands to the coast, terrorist violence, urban poverty, and cultural heterogeneity. In fact, there is nothing in the play that overtly references Peru; it takes place in ancient Thebes, and its plot and characters correspond directly to those of the original Greek tragedy. However, closer examination reveals that the play does relate to major themes in the Yuyachkani corpus, as it deals with issues such as the arbitrariness of power; the loss of social, cultural, and historical memory; the responsibility of the citizen; and the role of women in the maintenance of a national social conscience. Indeed, Peruvian audiences, regardless of their social or ethnic group or geographic location, clearly understood the play's metaphor of the post-conflict national situation when the play debuted in 2000.

A video of a performance of the play is available in the online digital library of the Hemispheric Institute (Grupo Cultural Yuyachkani).

Work Cited

Grupo Cultural Yuyachkani. *Antígona*. Directed by Miguel Rubio Zapata, 8 Jul. 2000. *Hemispheric Institute*, hemisphericinstitute.org/en/hidvl-collections/item/76-yuya-antigona.html.

Character List

In order of appearance:

NARRATOR

CREONTE

ANTÍGONA

GUARD

HEMÓN

TIRESIAS

ONE

NARRATOR[1]

Today is the first day of peace.
The enemy arms have yet to be collected, and they're
strewn about
over the dust, like useless offerings.
How quickly the morning breeze has erased the footprints
of the fleeing Argives.
When the light is as brilliant as it is this morning, the past
seems more remote.
But no, they fled just last night, no more nights than that.
Before we emerged from our slumber, they rushed away en
masse.
They came
and perched on our rooftops like armed eagles
and placed at our seven gates

seven renowned captains
never ceasing their sinister cries of war.
But Zeus, who loathes displays of haughty speech,
was with us.
Hounded by our battalions, they fled for their lives, those
 who were singing
that they had come to drink our blood.
They did not drink it, and today we give thanks for life
and the sun
and the peace that is a transparent air, and now let us begin
 to forget.

TWO

NARRATOR
The shepherds have taken the goats and sheep
beyond the hills of Thebes, where the grass
is not soiled by blood.
They will return when the war dead have been buried,
and new grass grows over the tumulus.
Make haste, gravediggers,
gather wisely in one same grave our soldiers and the enemy's
for both are made from the same flesh
and breathe the same air.
Do you see that cadaver on the driest land, laid out
perfectly on his side?
His name is Polinices and, though half-naked,

he still maintains the bright badges of an Argive captain.
He died from a perverse game of the gods.
They observe battles like spectacles, ignoring
who wounds whom in the clamor of combat
or which arrow heads toward a specific soul.
But at one of the seven gates,
the gods imposed their will so that two marked men would fight,
our captain Etéocles
and the assailing captain, Polinices.
Oh, perverse game:
two warriors with long lances stood staring, the one at the other,
rebuking each other,
each alone in his shining armor. Oh, perverse game,
born, as they were, of the same mother and the same father.
The move was simultaneous: one lance thrust forward and the other replied,
and thus death was split, yet became whole in each brother.

THREE

NARRATOR
It is the destiny of the weak to create masters of power,
just as in dreams we craft creatures for our fears, and only the slumbering one
sees them, and grows distressed.

But now I cannot sleep, and seeing Creonte frightens me.
Crowned yesterday, he is the freshest king of Thebes, and yet
his brow is already furrowed.
Slowly he descends his palace stairs and I know
no propitious words on are his lips.

CREONTE

Our country is once again a land of peace.
After the violent waves of war,
things have settled down and are functioning as before.
Look around:
there is wine in the amphoras,
servants shake out carpets from the windows,
love is nesting once again, and happily, for all, in the
immortals
and in the ephemeral men,
and the war dead are now all sheltered by the earth,
all but one.
All but one.
The body of Polinices will remain unburied, flesh
for voracious birds and dogs to fight over and stuff
themselves.
Because he, who was exiled, returned with the cruel Argives
bent to watch delighted as flames consumed the city of his
parents.
No tomb for him is my declaration

because the wicked will never receive more honor than
the just,
and may it thus be proclaimed.
And proclaimed as well be the punishment: whosoever
performs his funeral rites, mourns him or covers him with
earth,
will add his own death to that of the deceased.
Now let us conclude the honors for his brother Etéocles:
ready the carriages, horses, flowers, banners,
and you, war captains, add a lock of your hair
to be consumed with the body of the one whose cause was
the fatherland.
Let past combats thus remain forgotten
and let us go to the temples of the gods for nightly dances,
and may Bacchus be our guide!

FOUR

NARRATOR

The girl, more child than woman, seated in that patio . . .
what dejection so serenely borne.
Sister of the two deceased, the one honored with a tomb and
the other, defamed, with none,
looks from afar upon our passing. The guilt we feel is
within us, Thebans,
not in the intention of her gaze,

because no one, not even the wisest counselor, dared refute
Creonte's order,
so harmful to our soul.
What is burning in your heart, Antígona?
Whither does your outrage fly, young girl?
To Zeus, who has unleashed upon your family the whole
world's grief,
or to the king who now treats your brother with no mercy?

ANTÍGONA

A scepter, a throne, and honors, many honors all around
are with Creonte.
Oh, king, little did you need to start speaking with a tyrant's
voice.
No one knows the true heart of a man until seeing him in
power.
Before the war he strolled through this garden, whistling,
caressing
my, his niece's, head,
and then he'd disappear into the sunlit atrium. It was
another sun,
and I another niece.
This same man now orders that I rejoice in the Victory
and commit the unburied Polinices to oblivion
as if he were not my brother.
How can I go dancing and singing into the temples

if up on the hardest hill there lies a body without
    interment?
How can I toast, erasing from my eyes what they do not see
but certainly is?
It is a cadaver surrounded by guards, watched day and
    night
so that not even the wind can cover him with dust.
But if you are a dog or a bird of prey, you can reach him
and rend apart and gnaw the precious flesh
of my brother.
My brother, yet no longer my kin,
rather, everyone's corpse, tell me what to do.

FIVE

NARRATOR
The gods decreed you be born a woman, Antígona.
Little can you do but obey the laws, be they for the dead
or for those of us still living.
You have your heart set on ardent things, on disobedient
desires that would others freeze or turn
to statues from fear.
Rest, let your sleep be a peaceful truce
while the long night passes. Sleep.

Night falls, then comes dawn.

SIX

NARRATOR

The swift sandals of the guard,
who comes running down the shortcut through the hills,
are so swift
they seem to rush the light of dawn.
What message beats on his tongue, what news
upsets him in his race, what new calamity does he keep
in his shuttered words?
Now he climbs the humid palace steps,
now he has just enough breath to bid they announce him to
the king.

GUARD

How difficult it is for me to come to you, King, not owing to
the height of your power
but to my fear to give you the morsel I bring.
How many times I stopped along the way
because my heart would say, "Turn around, go back, careful,
for, no sooner do you share the news, you, yourself, will pay."
With such thoughts
the short trek became a long journey.
Yes, I know, I am talking to prolong my time,
and all I do is provoke your royal impatience.
So, let the news be told:
last night someone buried Polinices.

No, it is not that the deceased has found shelter under the
earth,
but that someone has rubbed fine dust over all his skin.
That someone, thus, began the burial rites,
but the light of dawn forced him to flee.
Guards against guards, we've blamed each other,
but, I ask you, could it have been the negligence of men, if
the one who disobeyed your decree
was a god?
That thought put an end to our discussion there on the hill.
Sire, you will agree, that whoever comes and goes
must leave a trace,
and there was none, from wheels nor feet nor scrape of a hoe.
Does not your heart tell you, as ours told us, that the
gravedigger came by air
or that he is not of visible human substance?

SEVEN

NARRATOR
At the gate of Boreas
the wind stirs like sad flags the rags of that man who,
captive, approaches.
Accused, he moves forward
while the dutiful guards drive him with their lances
and the mob encircles him.

They say he was prowling around Polinices's corpse
and that there was dirt under his nails.
There you have him, Creonte, the one who defied your order last night.
Are you going to judge him?
Laughable trial, king, or farce: How will you make him come to his senses
if the man is bereft of reason.
It is the crazy man who for years has been begging for alms by Amphion's monument.
Today, imprisoned, he cries that he was just in the hills to search for his dog.
His other voices
simply resound in his tormented mind, in his insanity
where there are no kings or heroes or traitors,
just simply a dog.

EIGHT

NARRATOR
I remember:
the poplar groves in spring
and Antígona ran and laughed like a little doe with her friends.
The only thrilling event
was their first menstrual blood, brilliant and clean,

and the only prophecy
was brought by the wind pinning their dresses to their
bodies, and announcing,
thus, full and desirable bodies.
Nothing foretold the somber young girl who now walks
alone under the pines
and leans her cheek on the rough bark so that nothing in her
can rest serenely.
The gods of the grove watch her pass, and not one of them,
from their marble,
consoles her.

ANTÍGONA

Oh gods, having been able to make us of an invisible
substance, or of stone
that needs no burial,
why did you shape us from matter that decomposes, from
flesh
that does not withstand the invisible force of putrefaction?
How shameless, how obscene
it is to end up unburied, exposing
inner flesh and viscidity to the eyes of the living. Such
punishment,
and worse, my brother endures
because he is also meat, torn apart by vermin, vultures,
and dogs.

Tall pines that saw me pass by when I was a child,
do you see my brother? Has the wind removed the
fine dust
with which I covered his nakedness at dawn?
Will I again find the courage to evade the redoubled
guard,
or should I resign myself to his body, at autumn's
approach,
being but bones and an oily stain upon the loose stones?
No, don't answer me. Today every word or murmur enters
my nightmare
and inflames it more.

Antígona gathers courage. Photograph by Elenize Dezgeniski.

NINE

Narrator

It was midnight,
and Creonte's palace seemed a safe and anchored ship.
The wind had subsided,
and the torches were being consumed under a still blue flame.
Contemplating the building, I pondered the ways of power:
a merciless man sleeps between silk sheets, I thought.
Suddenly
in the highest room, one light was lit and then another,
and I saw Creonte walking and walking, perturbed. Was he
awakened
by a bad dream
or the grief of mistrust that trembles on the skin of every
tyrant?

Creonte

The guard spoke with a superstitious tongue. Seeing no
footprints,
he and his fellow simpletons
suspected a divinity trying to bury Polinices's cadaver.
What god could trouble himself so
with one who arrived at the city gates carrying blazing
torches,
ready to burn down temples, altars, and sacred treasures?
Or have we reached the time when false gods

exalt traitors?
No: I see it now: the guard's stupidity was feigned,
and the gravedigging god a picaresque invention
to hide his paid complicity.
There are citizens resentful because they do not have a place
    at my side.
Eyes that I dispatch throughout the city
have seen them shake their heads and murmur diatribes
    behind my back.
The cadaver on the hill does not offend them; they are
    offended by my power,
and to erode it
they dropped coins into my guard's venal hand.
Yes, my sentry's daring and shameful scheme
Can only be explained by profit.
And then they tried to confuse me, like the naïve king of
    fables,
swapping a god for a madman who knelt before me
and proffered confused words while sobbing and drooling.
Power and betrayal are two sides of the same coin.
The day of my first command I met my first treason:
Polinices's death mask disappeared, the one
I made so that the enemy would have a face,
before it lost its features, as I ordered, under the sun.
Oh, traitors, tremble, because death alone will not suffice
    for you, either.

TEN

Narrator

I have seen Antígona running stealthily from one column to
another,
from one corner to another
as if hiding from no one.
Upon leaving through the gates of Boreas
her hurried white dress seemed to travel alone, like linen
waving on a line.
I lost sight of her when she entered the grassland,
but on her forehead she bore a thought that transfigured her
and made her more lovely in her fleet-footed walk under the
noonday sun.

Antígona

Polinices, my brother, you will ask how I have come to you.
Every man has his arrogance,
and that of the guards is believing that in such a luminous
hour, no one could be so bold.
I give thanks, as well, to the winds of the north
that curl up into whirlwinds and whoosh through the hills
stirring up columns of dust that ascend to the clouds.
Wrapped up in a whirlwind, I've arrived, covered in blades
of grass,
but the wine in the jug is clean.
How poorly did they scrape off the dust

that I sprinkled on you two nights past. For you they want
the most absolute exposure,
but I have come to open the earth for you.
Receive again over your body this consecrated dust
and these three libations of wine, from my mouth, but in
everyone's name.

A guard takes her by surprise.

Being caught was the risk I took, guard, but let me
finish opening this earth, so it may be a mother
and embrace Polinices like it embraced Etéocles.
They are undeniably brothers, guard, now without faction
or battle,
and perhaps are both now calling to each other.
In your heart you know
that it is not good that one be sheltered by the earth
and the other remain wandering,
a lost soul that regards his own cadaver with sadness and rage.
I want every death to have its funeral
and afterwards,
afterwards,
afterwards,
we forget.
Under your arrest, guard, my death is now beginning.
Remember my name

because one day everyone will say that I was the sister who
did not fail her brother:
my name is Antígona.

ELEVEN

Narrator

People of Thebes
who watch and hide like curious monkeys,
she who goes through the streets encircled by guards like
hunted prey
is in fact the only princess of this land.
Look at her now
climbing the palace steps: if her sandal straps are loose,
the cords on her sacred wrists
cut very deep into her flesh.
People of Thebes,
Antígona and Creonte have now assumed their inevitable
roles.
She takes her place as a prisoner,
and he is now not only king, but the strident voice of destiny
and its inclemency.

Creonte

You were born
of my sister's womb and a bond of love ties you to Hemón,
my son.

And so, you are more my kin than many.
Double the pain and double the rage burn in my soul.
It is just, then, that I am doubly harsh with you.
My son Hemón wanders incredulous through corridors and rooms,
knowing himself betrothed to a condemned woman.
Because you have been condemned from the moment the edicts proclaimed
the order and punishment.
And yet you laugh, and that insolence is worse than the burial
because there you fooled simple, unenlightened guards,
and here your sarcasm and disdain
are directed at your king.
It is always easier to order the death
of one who commits a crime and then assumes it as an honor. Your laughter
will make condemning you a pleasure as well.
But who else laughs with you?
What accomplices hide in their homes and delight in your audacity?
Ismene, your sister, did she, too, assist you; is she the other head of the bicephalous viper?

Antígona

The viper has but one head, Creonte.
My sister Ismene is innocent. Her most audacious thoughts

go no further than her timid brow.
You say I have broken your law.
Mortal, do you pretend to prevail
over the unwritten but unbreakable laws of the gods?
Only they have authority o'er the bodies of the dead.
Remember that: only they.
I know well
that Polinices came to lay waste to our country and that
Etéocles was defending it,
but now, both dead, Hades bestows on them equal rights.
As you see,
I have preferred to obey the gods and not your arrogant
whim.
To succumb for such a motive is a win, and does not
grieve me.
It would grieve me, yes, that the son of my own mother
remain unburied. You, keep calling him enemy
till the end of your days,
but I was born to love, not to share hatred.
You must think there is a ring of madness in my words,
but no, the madness is in your ears.
Do you know there are many Thebans who would proclaim
these same words,
who would shout them in the streets and plazas,
if fear did not shut their mouths?
May the gods will, Creonte,

that your privilege to order with impunity whatever pleases
you not last,
and may they also desire to quickly end your pleasure at
hearing
only multitudinous
and indignant
silence.

TWELVE

NARRATOR

Let's not suppose so much hardness in the heart of the king.
Surely he has conquered a thousand doubts before sentencing the girl
who made a promise of love to his son
and is so close to him by blood.
Oh, Antígona, what a comely and proud prisoner you are.
The escort guards
do not disturb your slow and regal
walk.
You look about unruffled
at the faces in the windows, trees, paths, the glint of sunlight
on a door latch, and a thousand things that for you will be
the last.
They do not take you to the gallows, to an end that swiftly
comes like the flight

of an arrow or the fall of an ax, no:
Creonte has sentenced you to a death all will remember, a
    death
thus proclaimed:
if so great a punishment he decrees for family, what can
    other enemies expect?
You are going, Antígona, to a most lengthy and perverse
    death.
Amidst the mountain's rocks, there are deep and capricious
    caves. In one of those will you be tossed
and thoroughly walled in.
It will be for you a prison,
while your interminable hours of hunger and thirst and
    darkness last,
and then, a secret and immense tomb, for not only will you
    be sheltered by the cave
but by the entire mountain.

THIRTEEN

ANTÍGONA

The darkness gives my body a strange existence.
I am
only when I feel myself or touch the hard rock of the cavern.
When I speak, I know not if I speak; perhaps they are only
    words that circulate

soundless in my mind.
This
and death
I must pay in this time of perverse confusions.
Mercy, which was once a virtue, now condemns me
and prolongs my family's misfortune.
The elders say that an ancient curse weighed upon my
father and my mother
and that misfortunes, like ocean waves, will be repeated
from one generation to the next.
And so from here, although you do not hear me, elders, I
remind you
of a law of Olympus
that says
that nothing great comes into men's lives
without some curse.
If peace is that great thing, I am the curse, the strange wave
that crashes and dies inside this cave.
I am sorry for you, beloved Hemón. We were a woman and
man who dreamed
of nuptial rites, banquets, and a wedding bed.
My beloved now will be another, he will emerge from the
darkness,
I will eat my feast, this air,
and I will lie down on this rock that on that last day will feel
like feathers.

FOURTEEN

NARRATOR

Since early morning
Hemón walks just to walk, he comes and goes
nowhere
and only stops to look at the mountain where Antígona is being consumed.
What has happened in my land
to make eyes so young gaze with so much bitterness?
Last night Hemón had a senseless dream:
he saw himself abruptly killed
by a golden arrow shot by some compassionate god,
and, thus pierced through and lifeless,
in dreams he entered the cave to seek among the shadows
the beloved shadow of his promised one.
Dawn's light told him he was dreaming, and he hated the light.
He arose and began to walk aimlessly: caring not
whether he stepped on grass, rocks, or gravel.
A question took full shape during his wanderings:
How far should love for one's father go? Must we pay
that debt of origin,
even if it means the silent acceptance of his injustices?
Hemón knows it is a rebellious question, but bears it in his expression

as he goes up to speak to Creonte.

CREONTE

My son, I heard rumor of your resentment at your frustrated wedding,
but look at me: I am king and father, but not two persons, one
inflexible
and the other soft.
My firmness at home must extend to all the corners of the land
where I should be obeyed in things small and things just,
and even in that which is neither.
Having children is a risk, Hemón.
Those who are weak of heart
are good only for the mockery of enemies,
but I have confidence in you, I gave you strong feelings,
and I know they cannot dissolve in your hunger
for the pleasure of a woman.
Know, as well, that the naked embrace of the one
who has behaved as an enemy of our kind
would be suspicious, if not frigid.
Let her find a bridegroom in Hades
and you, my son, seek among other damsels
other fields to plow.

HEMÓN

It is very strange to be the son of a powerful man.
I hear you utter a father's domestic words

alongside a king's laws and orders.
And I feel privileged not to see you
as the great leader who intimidates others.
I ask your permission to use that privilege,
and tell you what I hear in the streets, amongst the shadows:
the whole city weeps for Antígona.
Lowly citizens reprove the offensive death
to which you are condemning her. They say:
"She who would not let her brother become food for dogs,
isn't she more worthy of honor than punishment?"
Hear them, father.
I wish for you all the wisdom of the world, but the gods
have yet created such a man.
Do not mimic the arrogant men of a thousand talents[2] who
when cracked open
are hollow.
Listen to the lowly citizens, father.
Do not feel humiliated by learning from them.
May your laws not be of your sole discretion, because a
homeland
is not one sole man's possession.
And listen to the gods. Look at the night
because in the stellar silence,
they ask that you neither forget nor trample their rights over
the dead.
Listen to them all, father, and yield,

and revoke your harsh order so we may all celebrate the
peace,
and Antígona, the light.

FIFTEEN

Narrator

The lively goats skip from crag to crag,
and they mate
without suspecting that in the womb of the sun-soaked
mountain
there is a cave
that is a perpetual prison and tomb and wedding bed.
The sacred eye of day cannot pierce through,
nor can the weeping of friends and kin. In this silence
laborious death envelops the condemned young woman
in a dense cocoon of shadows.

Antígona

I tried to be the just burier
and to be buried is the reward I have reaped.
Father of mine,
mother of mine,
brothers Etéocles and Polinices, I now feel I can touch your
hands,
which you stretch out to me from the other world.
I will die without the nuptial songs

or a husband's caresses
or a child to raise. I could only be a grateful daughter and
    sister,
receive me as such.
Strange is my death. My young body
has no destructive or cruel infirmity,
and here I do not await the impossible blow of a blind sword
so I can die spilling my blood.
I am slowly expiring: whilst I consume life,
the sweet abandonment we call death
enters me
and grows.

SIXTEEN

NARRATOR
A stranger passing through Thebes
would see an orderly realm, a king who governs
and a people calmly laboring.
He would not see the turbulence below the still water.
Who would tell him
that a girl is dying for her piety?
Who would inform him
that the enraged young man who leaves the palace would
    tear off his own skin
if by doing so he would cease to be the son of the king?

And now we suspect that the secret undercurrents will grow stronger
because here comes Tiresias, the old seer: a bad omen
is his beleaguered gait, due not to his age but to the weight
of his presages.
The gods gave Tiresias a paradox:
they blinded him so he could see further,
and so he goes, trusting his steps to a guide, before Creonte.

TIRESIAS
You can allege, sire, that your throne rests on broad marble bases.
I see it at the edge of an abyss.
Hear me:
Things are happening that you should fear.
The thousand birds on my tree, chattering songbirds,
were forced out by great birds filled with rage
who made the tree a battlefield
where they cruelly brandished claws to bleed each other dry.
Not understanding that violence, perhaps
a prelude of more to come,
I ran to offer sacrifices at the altar. I put on the brazier
the usual offerings—fresh sheep and ox bones and small bladders
of bile—
all smeared with oil to stoke the fire,

but, oh, the fire did not raise its flames,
and the fat melted drop by drop over the embers producing
great smoke, and the bile
splattered the dark and poisonous air.
Tell me, Creonte, why did the gods reject my sacrifice?
And so it is in all of the altars, house by house
like a plague. And, as if following an order,
birds and dogs appear at the altar burners
and pack them with remains torn from Polinices's corpse.
Is my skill as a seer to interpret such signs needed, really?
You challenged the gods, but all of Thebes is paying for your
insolence.
I shall leave asking you to stop piercing the cadaver.
Bury it.
Let it be said that you were valiant in amending your error
and not in killing once again he who is already dead.

SEVENTEEN

NARRATOR
No one around. Creonte is sitting alone in the middle of the
great hall.
He regards himself in the mirror
and sees an irritated man drinking wine.
And no one around.
The wine is from the royal vineyards,

but his thoughts fall into the glass and the drink becomes sour.
And no one around.

CREONTE

Who is not against me?
Hemón, my son, dominated by a vile woman?
Tiresias, the aged seer, who blames me for the dead flames on the altars
without seeing the gods are fed up and no longer want the offerings of the faint-hearted?
Who is not shooting arrows at me?
Who would not trade me like merchandise if there were a buyer?
But once again I say: Polinices
will never be buried in a tomb
even if the eagles
tear scraps from his remains and carry them to the throne of Zeus himself.

EIGHTEEN

NARRATOR

Tiresias, the old man with dead eyes,
transforms his body into one enormous eye, to see not today's happenings
but rather tomorrow's.
Last night he could not fall asleep

and was seeing calamities
that time is quickly bringing towards Thebes.
As soon as he felt daybreak's sun on his aged skin
he placed a hand on the shoulder of his guide
and set out for the palace. He carries premonitions
frightening events
he can no longer keep from sharing.

TIRESIAS

Again I come before you, Creonte, to ask that you be
humbly silent
and that you listen to the arrival
of the Furies of Hades
and the gods. They approach
swiftly and vengefully, and you are their inevitable prey.
You, because you believe that your swelling power is
enough to govern other worlds.
You hold Polinices in the world below
though he belongs, like all dead, to the world above.
And in a contradictory game,
you have in a cave, that is a death tomb,
Antígona, who lays dying, yet is still alive.
Last night, images of your disaster came to me. I tried to
dispel them
by bathing my brow with cool water, but they returned
time and again. I saw

the terrible retribution of the gods: carrying among
themselves
a being sprung forth from your own being, the most
beloved one.
And even now as I speak to you
the smell of blood overcomes me, a precipitate stench,
perhaps of tomorrow.
Avoid, Creonte, the flight of the Furies, make them desist
from their revenge
and return to their worlds. Abandon your blindness,
which is worse than mine, because it is not of carnal eyes
but of arrogance,
and hear me:
you already know that counsel is greater when it keeps away
the worst of evils,
and that which I leave with you is among the greatest: bury
the dead man
and free his loyal sister, and do so soon
because with each hour
the blood that is coming for you smells nearer.

NINETEEN

Narrator

There is no worse torture than one's own imagination,
and Antígona will not leave my mind.

I see her waiting for an impossible drop of water to form
on the arid rock
and fall into her thirsty mouth,
or fumbling about in that inhospitable world for a bitter weed
for her infinite hunger,
or pronouncing laggard words so that her own voice keeps
her company
while surrendering to lethargy
doubling over like a wax figurine.

ANTÍGONA

She speaks as if far away while playing with a silk sash she has untied from her waist; she twists and untwists it on her arm.

I dreamt it was daybreak. How absurd,
I dreamt it was daybreak.
Perhaps the dawn is over this mountain,
but it will not have the resplendent light of my dream.
The light I saw was another,
and I wanted to enter it and dissolve into its lightness.
Oh, were this the road to enter Hades, and to be a flash of
light, a body fled from this long and perverse
nightmare.
Oh, that I could take that path, that quick door, that
shortcut.

TWENTY

Narrator

From early on
the royal clarions have called the people to the palace doors,
but the Thebans, before merely compliant, today
bring something to reproach. They will shout
that their altars remain useless, the fires drowned, as they are,
by Polinices's remnants.
But Creonte has surprised them. He has come to the atrium
with another face. No one knows if due to reason or to fear,
but he is like a fisherman who has spent all night
untying a hundred knots
and the next morning observes, satisfied and at peace, his
smooth line.
A hundred knots all night long, and no one knows if they
have been loosened
due to reason or fear.

Creonte

People of Thebes:
giving an order and then suspending it should not be a
government's custom,
but if said order brings such anxiety
and insisting on it
can doom the people and even me to misfortune,
it is time to revoke it.

You secretly hoped for this decision. May your hearts then
rejoice today
because I give you leave to go and bury the dead man.
Deliver to him,
in song,
his right to be covered by this, his native earth.
I will perform a divergent task. I will go to the mountain
to destroy the stony seal
that cloisters Antígona and separates her
from light
and the love of my son Hemón, who for days has been
avoiding my gaze.
Let us go right away,
and may the gods be pleased by seeing us thus work.

TWENTY-ONE

NARRATOR

The seal of stones was broken,
and the recently arrived Creonte, incredulous and offended,
saw the hole,
and focused all his rage
against the heavens and earth
in one sole query: "Who dared do this?" he shouted.
Through the opening, more the work of desperate claws
than human hands,

entered guards with torches and the king with his rage.
And, advancing towards the dark depths,
they heard an overwhelming lament. It was the voice
of Hemón,
but Creonte denied it, saying it was a cruel trick of the gods.
Did you also try to deny, king, the image the torches revealed?
Antígona hanging by her elegant neck, bound
by a red silk sash to an overhanging rock,
Hemón embracing her corpse at the waist, ruing
his delay in daring to break the seal.
When the young man felt the light, he turned his face, and
there was
more fire in his eyes than in the torches.
Rancor produces an acid froth, and with it
he soiled the face of his father
before attacking him with his double-edged sword. The son
only wounded the air, the empty space
left by the evasive and agile body of Creonte.
Foiled in his attack, Hemón raised his sword
and plunged it through the center of his own chest. A
ferocious sign
of ire against his own father.
Life stayed with him just as long as he needed to turn,
embrace Antígona,
and wet the pale cheeks of his betrothed with the blood
rising from his mouth.

Oh gods, on the walls of the cave, their shadows
were those of two youth united
as on their wedding day.

TWENTY-TWO

NARRATOR
The deaths in this story come to me
not so that I can tell the tale of others' misfortunes.
They come to me, and so vividly, because they are my own misfortune:
I am the sister whose hands were tied by fear.
Antígona entered my house like an irate and sudden brilliance
and spoke to me thus: "Ismene,
I want your hands to help me bury the body of our beloved brother,
I trust
that, having been born noble,
you have not been overcome by villainy."
Her words burned,
but I had the will of a small, cowering
animal,
and knowing she was right,
I told her she was delirious, that an air of madness had smitten her head.

It was fear, Antígona, because death would be our reward
for burying him.
Come, sister, I begged you, better we ask the dead to
forgive us
than to have the orders of living rulers prevail over us,
but you reproached me, saying, "Ismene, you seek
the approval of the tyrant's world, I will seek the grace
of the gods," and you left
for our dead one's hillside.

She opens a bundle and reveals the death mask of Polinices. During the pauses in her speech, she offers three libations.

Antígona,
do you see this world below?
The palace now has a profound, tomb-like silence
and from there it is a breathing corpse that governs us, a
tormented
king
who is quickly growing old.
My sister, look:
this is the face of our brother, before the dogs
and the vultures and the rot,
and these belated libations come from my small, guilt-
ridden soul.
In your kingdom above

The Narrator (Ismene) with Polinices's death mask. Photograph by Elsa Estremadoyro.

ask Polinices to forgive the duty I did not fulfill in time
because I was cowed by the scowl of power, and tell him
that I now bear a great burden:
to remember every day your gesture
that tortures me
and shames me.

END

Notes

1. In the Spanish original script, *Narradora* indicates that the narrator is female.
2. *Talent*—an ancient unit of weight of monetary value.

Santiago (2000)

Santiago, written in collaboration with Peter Elmore, takes place in an unnamed Andean town at the end of the Internal Armed conflict (1980–2000). In the play, the three remaining inhabitants prepare to celebrate the festival of the town's patron saint, Santiago (Saint James the Apostle), which involves the procession of a large platform carrying a statue of Santiago, mounted on a rearing horse, with a statue of a "Moro" ("Moor") lying beneath the horse's raised front hooves.[1] Also known as Santiago Matamoros, or Saint James the "Moor-slayer," according to legend, Santiago appeared in a ninth-century battle to help Christians defeat Muslim armies in their centuries-long Reconquista of the Iberian Peninsula.[2] The myth cemented Santiago as the Patron Saint of Spain and an icon of Spanish identity. Santiago was said to have reappeared in the Spanish conquest of the Americas, helping the Spaniards overcome Indigenous resistance. Known as Santiago Mataindios—Saint James the "Indian-slayer"—he was said to have led the Spaniards to victory over the Incas in Cuzco. As Indigenous Andeans converted to Christianity, the figure of Santiago was fused with Illapa, a powerful Andean deity of thunder and lightning.[3] Santiago-Illapa was both feared by and seen as a protector of Indigenous Andeans; Yuyachkani's *Santiago* draws on this syncretism.

This play centers around three characters: the Majordomo, or Mayordomo (don Armando)—the host or sponsor of a community festival—who also assumes the role of Santiago; the Indigenous Custodian of the church (Rufino), who is forced by the Majordomo to play the character of the Moro, when they cannot find the Moro statue for the procession; and Bernardina, a local townswoman whose twin sons have disappeared, likely killed in the recent Internal Armed Conflict. They are gathered in the town church, which, like many colonial churches, was originally built over a local *huaca*.[4] The Custodian, who lives in the church, observes Andean Indigenous spiritual beliefs and surreptitiously cares for the *huaca*. A large amount of the dialogue is in Quechua, without translation for non-Quechua speaking audiences, requiring the audience to work through the discomfort of not understanding the actor-creators Augusto Casafranca (Majordomo) and Amiel Cayo (Custodian), both fluent Quechua speakers, and to endeavor to capture the gist of the play's meaning through other visual and aural clues. In addition to the specific historical context and Andean cultural references in this play, Yuyachkani employs distinctly Quechua and Andean Spanish wordplays, double entendres, and verbal sparring in the rich dialogue between the three characters.

A video of a performance of the play is available in the online digital library of the Hemispheric Institute (Grupo Cultural Yuyachkani).

Notes

1. The play uses the terms "moro" ("moor") and "indio" ("Indian"), which are derogatory, racist terms first used in the Middle Ages to designate Muslims (particularly those from North Africa) and later, beginning in the fifteenth century, Indigenous peoples of the Americas. However, the terms are still widely used in a variety of cultural contexts throughout Latin America, from the beloved rice and beans dish "moros y cristianos" ("Moors and Christians") to popular festivals and

religious processions where characters representing these figures may have prominent roles. In *Santiago*, Yuyachkani draws on historical and contemporary popular uses of the figure of the "moro," fusing him with a character who also represents an "indio," in order to expose, criticize, and resist racial hierarchies in the Andes.

2. The Muslims had inhabited Iberia, then called al-Andalus, from the early eighth century to 1492. The final battle that consolidated Christian rule over the pennisula, the conquest of Granada, ended just before Christopher Columbus's first voyage, which was sponsored by the Spanish monarchs Ferdinand II of Aragon and Isabella I of Castille. Culturally and materially, the Reconquista influenced much of the subsequent invasion of the Americas.

3. St. James's association with thunder in the Christian tradition facilitated this connection for Indigenous Andeans. David W. Gade writes, "Santiago's lightning associations, while tangential to the Spaniards, made him a formidable deity to the Indian population" (778). Writing of the fusion of the two entities, Gade notes, "a major outcome of these culture-religious accretions was to reinforce attachments to indigenous beliefs. Simply by invoking Santiago, Indians were able to continue long after the Conquest to hold lightning-related ceremonies, fasts and vigils that resembled those of the Inca period" (779).

4. In Andean Indigenous cultures, a *huaca* (*Waka, wak'a* in Quechua) is a sacred object or place, such as a built memorial or an object in nature. During the conquest, Spaniards often built churches on top of important Indigenous *huacas*, to emphasize a spiritual, as well as political and military, conquest of the region.

Work Cited

Gade, David W. "Lightning in the Folklife and Religion of the Central Andes." *Anthropos*, vol. 78, nos. 5–6, 1983, pp. 770–88.

Grupo Cultural Yuyachkani. *Santiago*. Directed by Miguel Rubio Zapata, 2001. *Hemispheric Institute*, hemisphericinstitute.org/en/hidvl-collections/item/116-yuya-santiago.html.

Character List

In order of appearance:

MAJORDOMO / SANTIAGO

CUSTODIAN / MORO / UKUKO

BERNARDINA

ONE

Bernardina, the Majordomo,[1] *and the Custodian are in the church, which is closed, abandoned, and filled with piled-up pews and statues of saints. They repeatedly approach the chapel that houses the statue of Santiago, trying to open it in vain. They dust and sweep, arrange the pews and statues in their places, and light lamps and candles. Bernardina and the Majordomo exchange furtive glances each time they observe the Custodian. They sing to the saints, but this ends in an argument between the Majordomo and the Custodian about the keys to the chapel.*

The Majordomo grabs a bottle and serves himself a drink. He raises the glass to the statue of Santiago, pours some of the liquor on the ground, and starts to drink. For the entire play, he continues to drink and becomes progressively more inebriated.

MAJORDOMO: Kusa, kusa allinmi tukachichkanki chay violiniykita. Hinaspa kunan willawaykuyá, ah? Maypim kachkan chay llawita, qam yachankich, riki.[2]

CUSTODIAN: Ima llawita qantaq quwankimanchá, tata curata maskhay, pay yachanmi maypitaq llawi.[3]

Throughout the scene, it is obvious that the Custodian must have the keys.

MAJORDOMO: Maypis chay tayta cura? Manañam kaypiñachu, maytach ripuran, pasakapuran, qamtam qurasunki chay llawita.[4]

CUSTODIAN: Manam, kay llawita tatayqa quwanmi ñuqapaqmi, qayna punchawmanta yanqataq turiyawachkankitaqmi.[5]

MAJORDOMO: Manam hinachu, llullam kanki, yaw, taytayki hina; qanra runam kanki, sutuchi hina. Papayki hinam kachkanki, kay runakuna hinam (*Pointing out to the audience*) indium kanki, ¡indio![6]

CUSTODIAN: Qamtaq kanki llulla, qanra; ñuqawantaq hapinakuyta munani, hinaspa? Hamuy hamuy, ah.[7]

MAJORDOMO: Upallay simiykita yaw, indium kanki.[8]

The two characters keep arguing, and little by little the scene changes. The Majordomo goes over to the saint's chapel and the Custodian moves behind the horse. The argument dies down.

TWO
Dream

Bernardina falls asleep and dreams. Music signals that they all travel imaginarily through time, to an atemporal moment. The Majordomo and the Custodian are transformed into Santiago (Saint James) and a Moro. Santiago is sitting atop a large horse statue and the Moro is crouched underneath its hooves, on the platform. Bernardina is witness to their conversation.

Moro: Rider of a dwarf mule, you should be, and not of a good horse. Why do you insist on mounting, anyway, if you're just going nowhere?

Santiago: What do you know if I'm going, staying, or coming?

Moro: Come, you say? I'd come to blows with you, but even disemboweling you wouldn't be quite enough.

Santiago: I was talking about coming back, you stupid Moro, and you know it.

Moro: Where are we coming from, after so much time? From the first place where we fought, or perhaps the last?

Santiago: I no longer have any memory of the first. Of the last one, yes, and rather fresh. I beat you near the hot springs, in Cajamarca.[9]

MORO: That's a lie. You beat Indians there and called them "Moors." You can't fool me so easily; how well I know your cunning ways.

SANTIAGO: *Your* cunning, you wretch. Where have you put your statue? At what careless point in my dreams did you find the chance to hide it? You know well that my faithful want to parade me about my lands, to let the air from my incense cleanse the town. But the platform needs to carry your dead weight as well. Otherwise, the procession is not complete.[10]

MORO: My secrets are not for you. Had I had his ear, I would have told the Inca king who you are. Fortunes would have flowed differently that afternoon if I had talked to him.

SANTIAGO: What flowed was the blood of your troops. In that river I saw floating the color of your hide. When the gentiles lost, you lost, too.

MORO: We have been fighting for centuries. For how long do you want to keep me under you, choking down dust and sucking up your bodily secretions? Don't you think it's been enough already?

SANTIAGO: Only one order rules the four corners of the winds. There must be a below because there is an above: the procession has to show that.

MORO: And who will see it, you arrogant saint? Only three souls remain, and not one more, in this town.

SANTIAGO: I am Saint James the Greater—first martyr of Jerusalem, Captain of the high heavens and Grand Master by the will of the Lord of the Blue Field of Stars.[11] No matter where I am, my power shines equally bright.

MORO: Power? Come down here, then, and show me if you are as tough as me.

The Moro pulls out a little sack and strews broken glass onto the floor. Dancing, he first lies face up and then stands on his head on top of the shards, flaunting his resistance to pain. Santiago dismounts the horse and laughs disdainfully.

SANTIAGO: So, this is how you have fun? (*He grabs a fistful of glass and eats it. On finishing, he turns to the Moro.*) Come, then, crouch down and lock your hands, so I can get up in my saddle again.

The Moro thinks about it a moment and then, indeed, helps him onto the saddle. He spins the platform around. Santiago orders him to stop, but the Moro pays him no mind.

MORO: You can think of nothing better than to humiliate me. Gentle sir, is this how you like to ride?[12]

SANTIAGO: You are going to howl, you abandoned animal, you are going to howl when I tear out that tongue, Satan's dog.

Moro (*Spinning the platform rapidly*): Dog, no. You are the dog and your soldiers . . . more dogs. Without a horse to sit on or thunder in your pulse, you would no longer be Santiago. Liar, you are to lie in dust.[13]

He stops abruptly.

Santiago: Moro! There is no mercy with you nor will there ever be! Broken-colored piece of trash![14] Bite the Patron Santiago, bite me if you can.

The Moro does some acrobatic movements, as if warming up for a fight. Santiago begins to come down from the horse; from the platform he addresses the Moro.

Santiago: That's how you respond, with dancing tricks? Come, if you're a warrior. Dare to enter where my shadow falls.

The Moro throws himself on Santiago.

Santiago: It's a duel you want? You're looking to measure yourself against me?

Moro: I want a fight, without steel or saddles.

Santiago: So be it, with arms and legs. No other weapons.

They both fight violently, and Santiago almost destroys the Moro, but in the end he spares him. Santiago wins the struggle and, with a push, situates the Moro under the horse.

Santiago: May this also be your effigy when my faithful leave the church.

Moro: I don't know if I want to remember where my statue is. Or, maybe I'm going to find it right now.

Santiago: Stupid Moro, I will have to follow your steps, although I know well that you are speaking with malice. (*They both retire.*)

The Majordomo places the Moro, played by the Indigenous Custodian, under the horse statue for the ritual procession. Photograph by Elsa Estremadoyro.

THREE
Bernardina's Monologue

Bernardina has witnessed everything and becomes anxious upon seeing the Moro leave. She awakens and converses with the statue of the Saint, while she carries an immense candelabra. The Custodian plays the violin, while the Majordomo moves the horse.

BERNARDINA: Heavenly Patron? Patron Santiago, are you there? We've been here all afternoon already, searching, waiting, cleaning, and your things have not been found. It's been fifteen years since we've taken you out, papáy, but not in bad faith. How could we forget you? I don't even need to tell you: you know everything, from your heights you have surely seen us, into our deepest hidden depths you have certainly looked.

Help us, shine your light upon us so we can find what is missing. Your clothes aren't here, nor are the keys to your chapel. We don't know where the statue of the Moro is. Could it be that you don't want to process? Are you angry? When you go out, Patron, you bring so many blessings. The children are happy when they see you mounted on your white horse; they run behind you, like my sons ran in their day. Do you remember, Patron, do you remember?

Now, filled with fear, my chest tight, I enter your church. Below, in its foundation, people say the huaca is alive, but I still dare to enter, Patron. I dare to ask you for help. Won't you use your strength to help us?

The war has ended, but when will peace come? We are worse off than ever, like blindmen. Before, people respected authority. The war brought controls, permissions. Everything was being watched, on lists. We knew how many of us there were, who left, who came, how many animals, how much food. There was even an edict for the loose women who hung around the troops, the officers. Every need, high or low, had an answer.

Of course, there was death and pain, but I knew how to live there.

Night is falling, the winds blow, the doors tremble.

What I feel is like a bad dream. Could it be true, Patron, that I have seen you, agonizing with rage, fight your enemy? Just, just like that, hating each other deeply, my twin boys fought here, too.[15] So hard, they drew blood from each other. As if they had not spent nine months together in my womb. And then, without leaving an address for me to send a parcel, they left me. I come to you, Patron, not for me, for them. Beautiful Knight, Just Lord, Taita Santiago, Ruler of these High Heavens and Caves![16] I ask you for the gift of the return of my sons, Patron. I promise to adorn you, ready your platform, hold vigil, and take you out in procession now and forever, Patron, now and forever!

FOUR
The Rite

The Majordomo has moved the horse to see what is behind it. He enthusiastically summons the Custodian to help him lift the cross. They push it and are able to open a small door underneath the cross from which they extract a parcel wrapped in a woolen shawl. Bernardina grabs it and tries to open it. After a struggle, the Custodian, who is always resisting what is going on, snatches it away from her. Without realizing what has happened, the Majordomo calls Bernardina to give her another parcel, which contains the horse's saddle wrapped in a shawl. She takes it to the center of the church, while he brings with him an old suitcase. Together, Bernardina and the Majordomo open the suitcase; the Majordomo extracts some cloth, revealing the Saint's mantle.

MAJORDOMO: Finally, the Saint's vestments.

BERNARDINA (*Looking at the Saint's chapel*): Thank you, beautiful, dear Father! (*Addressing the Custodian*) You see, the Saint *does* want to process.

CUSTODIAN (*Opening the parcel he had taken from Bernardina*): Mama kukata tapusun sichus patronniykita lluqsiyta munan.[17]

Bernardina and the Majordomo begin to arrange everything to prepare the platform while the Custodian begins a parallel rite that leads him to another state of consciousness. He becomes an intermediary for the spirits of the huaca.[18] *Bernardina takes initiative and begins to clean and adorn the Saint. The Majordomo tries to take the Saint's saddle away from Bernardina, who defends herself.*

Bernardina: We are going to bring out the procession together, so we need to dress him together.

Majordomo: Dressing and mounting is the Majordomo's job. You, madam, clean and adorn the platform.[19] (*He grabs the saddle from her.*)

Bernardina: All my life I've had to clean people's filth; I'll die cleaning, no doubt.

Majordomo: Why are you talking about dying, Bernardina? Each of us has to our own job to do; just wait until we bring out the procession. We'll recover our prestige, and we'll receive many blessings.

Bernardina: Where could the statue of the Moro be? Do you know? The Knights of the Brotherhood of Santiago told me that one night they heard noises in the church, like an argument or a fight, and then they saw the shadow of the Moro running away, towards the sea. As if he were going to his homeland, never to return. That's what they told me.

During this dialogue, the Majordomo has been working, polishing, and saddling the horse, preparing it for procession. Bernardina brings a bundle of flowers and a bucket with water, and begins to adorn the platform.

MAJORDOMO: This man knows something about the Moro, and also about the key, but he doesn't want to tell us. But he *will* talk, señora. The road to heaven is paved with patience and cheerfulness.

Bernardina looks at the Saint in the chapel and then at the Majordomo saddling the horse.

BERNARDINA: Don Armando, you look *just* like the Saint!

MAJORDOMO: Don't flatter me with flowery praise, Bernardina; best leave the flowers for the Patron Saint.

BERNARDINA: I was talking about your looks . . . (*She laughs*) because you've done nothing *just* in your whole life.

MAJORDOMO: Better we don't discuss our lives, señora, because you'd come out the loser. Besides, that's why we're here, to begin anew.

BERNARDINA: Rufino, what are you doing? Look for the keys to the Patron's Chapel. Where could Taita Priest have put them? I'm almost finished with the adornments and you're not doing a thing! What are you doing? What's this? This isn't Godly!

The Custodian, possessed by the huaca, has been sketching on the floor with chalk, creating an enormous copy of the drawing of the altar of Qoricancha, by the Andean chronicler Juan de Santa Cruz Pachacuti Yamqui Salcamaygua.[20] *When he finishes, he draws two star-lined paths, one that connects the altar of Qoricancha with the cross and the other that connects it with the chapel that holds the statute of Santiago, as if reclaiming and taking possession of both.*

BERNARDINA (*Crossing herself*): What's this? This is not of God!

Bernardina grabs a rag and with a broom starts to erase the drawing. Trying to grab the broom, the Custodian pushes her, and Bernardina falls down. The Majordomo jumps off the platform and starts punching the Custodian. Bernardina, desperate, frightened that they are fighting in the church, separates them. The three look at each other, frozen. Illapa responds—at that moment, thunder erupts, and the rain begins.

FIVE
Santiago Illapa

MAJORDOMO: Imataq kayri taytáy Santiago, imaraykum . . . [21]

CUSTODIAN (*Pointing out the radiance of the thunder*): Chaytam Illapap siñalninta, hawapi purikuchkanmi, kancharichkanmi, chaskichkawantaqmi![22]

BERNARDINA (*Running towards the front door of the church*): Why is it raining, Patron? It's the cold season; it never rains at this time. How are we going to do the procession? Patron Santiago, (*She approaches the cross and signals to the statue of the Virgin Mary*) Holy Virgin, Taita Jesus Christ, why is it raining? Why? Could it be the Patron doesn't want to process?

The Majordomo takes out a quena,[23] *then an accordion, which he gives to Bernardina.*

MAJORDOMO: Taytáy kunan punchaw, kaykamaraq hamuniku huñunakunanchikpaq, llapan llaqtakunapi yasta kachkanku qari warmikunapas, hinaspa kay sumaq takichata apachimuniku qamrayku tukuy sunqunchikwan.[24]

Bernardina plays the accordion and sings "Apu Jesucristo."

Apu Jesucristo
Kuyaq sunqu tayta
Khuyapallayaway
Waqcha wawaykita.[25]

The Majordomo accompanies her, first on the quena, and then singing. The Custodian, still possessed, undresses and climbs onto the cross, also singing "Apu Jesucristo," and assumes the position of the crucified Christ. The Majordomo sees him. The Majordomo and Bernardina, furious at the disrespect, begin to beat the Custodian with their shawls and then pull him down from the cross.

MAJORDOMO: Yaw, indio upallay simiykita, . . . lluqsiy chaymanta. Sutuchi uya.[26]

BERNARDINA: How dare you! Put your clothes on, get down! This is the House of God.

CUSTODIAN (*Taking command for the first time*): Kaypitaq Illapapa wasinmi, ñawpaq kutiqa hanaq pachamanta kay pampataqa chayamun, hinaspa huk rumi kanchata hatarirqamun; chay rumi kanchata, kay templomantaq kutichirqamun. Kaypim Illapapa espiritun yachanmi, Wiraqucha taytallanchikwan, Inti taytanchikwan; chaymantaraqsi Santiagum yuraq kawalluntin chayamun.

Chay k'ancharichkanmi, Illapam; parataq Illapam, q'ihutaq Illapam. Aswan Mama kukata willawachkanmi, Illapataq hawapi yachansi, manam procesionta munanmanchu; kamikuchkanmi, chiqnikuchkanmi, may ima rurayta manam allinmi kachkan, kay wataqa tikrasqa kachkan.[27]

Upon seeing how the Custodian expresses himself, and seeing that the Majordomo is listening to him while having a drink, Bernardina decides to continue arranging the flowers on the platform, attentive to what is happening.

MAJORDOMO: Upallay simiykita yaw maqta, astawan castiguta apachimunki.[28]

CUSTODIAN: Imam castiguta ñuqa apamusaq? Qamta astawan castigun chayasunkimanmi, kay llaqtaykita faltamuranki.[29] Besides, you're taking advantage of this woman's pain, because her sons are not going to return.

MAJORDOMO (*Addressing the guard*): That's a lie! I haven't taken this woman's bread, nor that of the orphan in times of war. I've kept the donations in my warehouses to better distribute them when necessary. I've sweat blood and tears to earn the trucks in my fleet, one by one. Without my help, who would come here, who would leave? (*Addressing Bernardina*) I am asking: for my troubles, don't I, too, deserve a reward? (*Bernardina turns away. The Majordomo looks at the cross and approaches it.*) My shawl warms our Lord, too. (*He tosses the shawl up on the cross.*)

Me, I show myself as I am. I'm not lying here. How could I lie here? I am strained, dirty, but I clean off my filth before entering your house, Lord. I've had to make my way by trekking through mud. How could I not end up like a filthy pig? I'm no saint . . . that's true. Patron Santiago is.

Here, everything's upside down. This horse is lacking its rider; this urn is lacking its keys. My two hands are not enough to count the years during which the Patron has not been able to solemnly process. For that, I blame myself. I have two faces: one I show to the world, and the other with which I look down at the foot of your cross. I accept your rage, Lord, but you won't let me mend my ways.

(*Grabbing the shawl, he hangs upside down on the cross, humbling himself before Christ, like Saint Peter.*[30]) Hanaq pachamanmá rillaymanmi taytáy, qam munasqaykim: munay wiqiy mana tanisqa kiriy . . . [31]

Listen to my promise, Lord: For each time that there was no solemn procession on the Saint's days, I will compensate seventy times seven with ten percent interest, and more even. Today, no matter what, we'll take the platform out for procession. My position, I offer you. My name itself—I will deny it if I don't fulfill my promise. (*He comes down from the cross's platform and begins to blow out the candles in the holder dedicated to the cross.*)

BERNARDINA (*Rinsing flowers and talking to herself*): In our community they said that children born during a storm were sons of Illapa. If they were twins, they killed one for Illapa and the other had to become a layq'a.[32]

It stops raining.

MAJORDOMO: The rain! Finally, the rain has stopped! Look, doña Bernardina!

BERNARDINA: Surely, the Lord must have heard your prayers.

Majordomo: Kunanmi upyaykusun, hapiy señora.[33]

Bernardina rejects the drink.

During the previous dialogue, the Custodian has been dressing up as an ukuko, a trickster character that wears a bearskin-like coat.[34]

Custodian-Ukuko: I'm going. There's nothing for me to do here. (*He puts on the white wool ukuko mask and tries to leave, but the Majordomo detains him.*)

Majordomo: You will leave here the right way . . . (*Mimicking the characteristic high pitch of the ukuko character*) "I'm going, I'm going . . ."

Custodian-Ukuko (*Using a typical ukuko falsetto*): Manan papituy lindu, nuqan pasapunaymi kashan, Q'uyllur Rit'iman puriykunallaymi kashan, amaña hark'awaychu.[35]

The Majordomo blocks the Custodian as he prepares to leave, acting nice and pretending to be his friend.

Majordomo: Yaw, maymantaq ripunkiri, maytam pasapunki chay sumaq uyachaykiwan. Kusa, allinmi ah, hinaspa Q'uyllur Rit'iman rinaykipaq kayta apamuni. Malliykuyyá ah, . . . misk'illañam ñuqa hina. Kaymanta ninkutaq, sumaqmi nispa.[36] (*They both toast with the aguardiente and make an offering to Mother Earth.*) Hinaptin kunan willawaykuyyá ah, maypim kanman chay llawi maskachkanikutaq, riki.[37]

Custodian-Ukuko: Llawita, nishaykitaq, tata cura apakapun, nuqa manan rikunichu.[38]

Majordomo: Maypas chayta manam qawankimanchu. Punkutan riki qhaway, imam warkurqamuchkan chaypi? Candadum, hinaspa maypim kanman chay llawi, yanapawayyá.[39]

Custodian-Ukuko: Hamuy, hamuy willasaykitaqmi, qanpaqlla; kaypipas altar mayor, hinaspa kay larupi tiyanmi mamitanchis María, kay chawpipi tiyashan Tatitun Jesucristo. Kunanqa, pin tiyashan kay larupi? Tata San Pedro, pay yachan maypim llawitaq, kunan payman tapuriy, ha.[40]

Majordomo (*He plays dumb and says ironically*): Chiqaqmi yawpuni, chay San Pedro hatun guardián, qamtaqmi huch'uy guardián kanki, hina kaptin, maypim kanman llawi kunanyá? Tapuy taytanchikta: "maypim llawita?" nispa.[41]

Custodian-Ukuko (*Scoffing*): Nuqachu tapusaq San Pedruman? Allin, allin. San Pedrooo, llawita apamuyy, kay runaqa munashan llawi. Manan uyarinchu, ruqt'um kashan riki, machullanña kashan riki.[42]

MAJORDOMO (*Now angry*): Maytapas siqamuy, hinaspa llawita apamuway.[43]

The Custodian-Ukuko gets up on the horse and from there calls to San Pedro and, with a derisive gesture, throws the key to the ground.

MAJORDOMO: Sshh, upallay! Señora, uyarirankichu? Chaymi llawi chaykunata rantimurani qullqiywan.[44]

BERNARDINA: That's what you think . . . Can't you see he's making fun of you? (*To the Custodian-Ukuko*) Get down from there!

MAJORDOMO (*Picking up the key*): This is the key! Now we're going to open this door. Come, doña Bernardina, help me. Kunanmi kay punkuta kichasun.[45]

The Majordomo opens the lock to the Saint's chapel, removes the chain, and opens the gate. Bernardina and the Majordomo contemplate the Santiago statue, then raise him up on their shoulders. Following the starry path drawn out earlier by the Custodian, they almost set the Saint down on the altar of Qoricancha, but they realize their mistake and carry him to the center of the church.

SIX
The Procession

The Custodian-Ukuko delivers the following monologue as the Majordomo and Bernardina remove the Saint from his chapel, clean, and prepare to dress him.

CUSTODIAN-UKUKO (*Addressing the horse, jokingly*): Chayqá, caballiruyki lluqsimun, kunanmi paqtataq qusunkiman.

Kaypipas sayaspa kashanki, manachu sayk'uranki? Icha china kawallullata munashanki.

Yarqasunkichu? Hamuy kay q'umir q'achuta mikhuy, chaytá wiksaykitaq thanta lata hina qaparishanmi, kay

Bernardina and the Majordomo dress the Saint. Photograph by Elsa Estremadoyro.

t'ikata mikhumuy, caballeruyki sillakuyta munan, waq tatitukuna manam ima kawallutapas munanchu. Paskaspa Q'uyllur Rit'iman pusaykuwanki nuqaman?[46]

Bernardina and the Majordomo place four benches around the Saint, blocking the entrance of the ukuko. While they leave the Saint sitting in the middle, they dress him with his luxurious cape, wig, hat, and sword. The ukuko reacts to each action. He runs about, is frightened, hides, and fires his slingshot in the air. The Majordomo and Bernardina finish dressing the Saint, while the Custodian-Ukuko rolls about on the ground, spinning around, erasing the drawing, thus once again hiding the ancient spiritual practices. The Majordomo places the Saint on his shoulders and, standing tall, with the cape on, we see an immense Santiago. The Saint rises (with the Majordomo underneath) and walks toward the horse. Bernardina makes way for him and together with the Majordomo, they manage to mount the Saint on the horse while the Custodian-Ukuko rolls about in the floor. The ukuko hears sounds of horses and harquebuses, that gradually mix with machine guns and helicopters. Amazed, he lifts his wool mask. Bernardina and the Majordomo place the Saint on the horse and finish adorning the platform, while the Custodian walks balanced on the backs of the benches.

Custodian: Imaraykum kay Patronninchikta hinata rikuspa kayta yuyani? Chiqatapuni runakunataq ninsi may unay wataqa, kay llaqtata millay runakuna chayamun, Patrón

Santiagum hina, kawallu sillakuspa escopetata tuqyachispa. Hinata ninsi Patrun Santiagum, Sunturwasipi, puyu pólvora patapi rikurikamun, gentilkunatas wañuchirqamun, ichu hinataraq rawrachimun. Haykapmantam wañuy? Haykapkamallam? Hinam kunan wataqa ñuqa allintam rikuni, ima qari-warmikunataq, sunqun chiqnikuspa, kay templuta yaykumun, sunqun chiqnikuspa, metralletata hapispa, dinamitata tuqyachispa, alcaldetata wañuchirqamun, teniente alcaldelta wañuchirqamun, teniente gobernadortawan wañuchirqamun, jueztawanmi riki, chayrayku taytacura manam hamunchu, soldadollataq hamun "vamos a matar al enemigo" nispa, chaymantaraqsi kay llaqtapi mana pipas yachanchu.[47] (*He jumps down, sits on the prie-dieu, and dreams.*) Kaypipas taytaypa tullunta pampasqa kachkan, "Suwa kanki" nispa, taytayta wañuchirqamun, manam taytay hina kaypim wañusaqkuchu.[48]

SEVEN
At Dawn

BERNARDINA (*To the Majordomo, while finishing up the adornments*): Dawn is breaking now. We have to start the procession, even if we don't have the Moro!

MAJORDOMO: Manam, no, Señora. The Patron Saint Santiago mounts his horse because the Moro is underneath. Besides, the Moro hears what the Saint doesn't.

BERNARDINA: The Patron will understand. Why wouldn't he? When the procession goes out, no one looks at the Moro. Everyone prays to the Saint and begs him for favors.

MAJORDOMO: It's not worth asking anything of the Patron if he is alone. I won't allow it! (*Looking at the Custodian*) The Moro is essential.

CUSTODIAN (*Lying down, delirious*): Manam! Manam taytayqa suwataq karanchu.[49]

BERNARDINA: Why don't we ask him to consult the coca leaves?

MAJORDOMO (*With a complicit, negative shake of the head*): Better not. Don't you see? The more this man dreams, the more he remembers. (*Addressing the Custodian with tenderness, while pushing and persuading him*) Yaw Rufinucha, amaña llakikuychu, sichus patronninchikqa yuyachisunki, hinaspa yuyachikuyyá, tapuy—maypim kanman chay Moro, rimay.[50]

CUSTODIAN: Patronniykita tapuriy ah; pay yachanmi maypitaq kachkan chay escultura moro nispa.[51]

MAJORDOMO: Arí, Patroninchik uyariwanmi, ichaqa manam rimapawanchu, ichaqa qamyá willachikuy.[52]

CUSTODIAN: Pichá apakapun? Icha sapallan pasakapun.[53]

MAJORDOMO: Maypas chay escultura estatua nisqanku, sapallanchus ripunman, pasakapunman.[54]

CUSTODIAN: Runataq hinata ninsi, Moro huk punchaw, sapallan sayaykakamun, hinatas pasakapun, icha suwa suwarakapun.[55]

MAJORDOMO: Yachankim, ama llulla kaychu. Willaway maypim estatuata suwa aparakapuran; hina kaptin suwakunamanta rimarisun, taytaykimantawan.[56]

CUSTODIAN: Qam yachawaqtaq allinmi, manachu qamtaq mayordomo kanki? Kay templo llawita qamtaq hapichiranki, icha qam suwa lawrun kankitaq.[57]

MAJORDOMO: Arí, mayordomom kani, ichaqa imaymanatam yachani, qammanta, taytaykimantawan. Kunanmi, aswan kaymanta rimarisun: cuartu kuchuykipi kaytam tarirani. ¿Imam kay? Rimay.[58] (*He takes from his pocket a stained red rag and throws it at the sleepwalker.*)

CUSTODIAN (*Rising, awake and surprised*): This belongs to señora Bernardina's sons. (*He approaches Bernardina and hands her the red rag, which is from Shining Path.*) Your sons have played with fire, with filth, too. Better get used to seeing them in your memories, and not in person.

BERNARDINA (*Trembling, she takes the rag, in her hands, raising it to her ears, then tosses it far away*): Iskay uya—Two-faced! Qincha—Malagüero kanki.[59] My sons will return. How could the Saint not come through for me?

MAJORDOMO: That's why we must come through for the Saint, as God wills! . . . And you, tell us, where is the Moro? You must know.

CUSTODIAN (*Looking at the woman and the Majordomo*): How many had to come down for you to rise up, don Armando?

MAJORDOMO (*Taking the ukuko mask off the Custodian's head*): Have you also lost the key to your brains?

Custodian: Have you also buried your memories? Do you really not remember all the corpses you've tossed into your truck, like debris?

Bernardina: Corpses? Were my sons there?

Custodian: Arí. Yes.

Majordomo: It's so easy to accuse, damned Indian!

Bernardina: Armando! Think well and hard before answering me: Is what this man says true?

The Majordomo hesitates, but upon seeing the Custodian withdrawing, he lies.

Majordomo: Your sons are alive, señora Bernardina, and they are going to return! By the grace of Patron Santiago, if we honor him as God commands. (*Glaring straight at the Custodian.*) With a complete procession.

Bernardina (*Hesitating*): With a complete procession.

Custodian (*Defiantly*): Arí, chunka pichqayuq wata patronniykiqa manam procesiunta lluqsinchu. Kunanmi lluqsimunantaqa munankichik? Manam lluqsimunmanchu, yachanaykipaq. Apamuy waqulluyta, sumaqllamanta mañakapusayki.[60]

Majordomo: Kaytachu munanki? Hinaspa pampamantayá huqariy.[61]

The Majordomo throws the Custodian's mask on the ground. While the Custodian retrieves the mask, the Majordomo takes one of the

Custodian's whips and treacherously attacks him. They both engage in a duel in the style of the Yawar Mayu.[62] *The Custodian manages to throw the Majordomo to the ground, and the latter asks Bernardina for help. Bernardina hesitates, but finally brings a rope and helps the Majordomo knock the Custodian out. Between the two of them, they subdue the Custodian to tie his hands. They secure the Custodian and put him on the platform in place of the Moor. The Custodian regains consciousness and cries out; he defends himself, cursing in Quechua, repeating the words he was uttering to himself while drawing earlier. They take him on a procession around the church. As they are about to take him out through the main door, a lightning storm and thunder erupt outside the church. The platform becomes increasingly heavy. Bernardina and the Majordomo try to push it but can't. The Custodian breaks loose, jumps off the platform, goes to the door of the church, and closes it.*

EIGHT
Return to the Dream

The music from Bernardina's opening dream is heard. Everything is getting dark; Bernardina lights a candle and sees the Majordomo-Santiago and the Custodian-Moro. All three walk around in different, opposing directions.

Moro: We have been fighting for centuries. For centuries, I've been kept down below, choking down dust and sucking up your bodily secretions, but my belly remains hardier than that of whales or griffins.

SANTIAGO: Lord, how much time has passed! It wasn't like this before.

MORO: What did you say? I couldn't hear you well.

SANTIAGO: How much time has passed. I really would have liked to process solemnly, but how can I do so without your image? You must be happy to avenge your destiny in some way.

MORO: I'll be happier yet when our fight is finally over.

SANTIAGO: Night is weighing on my eyelids, and on my entire body, all the time that has passed.

MORO: I've lost count of all the processions; today's would have been the next to last.

SANTIAGO: They're all next to last until Judgment Day comes.

MORO: And you don't know when that could be?

SANTIAGO: It's a secret even for me, but my bones know that that day is quickly approaching. When it comes, this imprisonment will finally end.

The woman turns to the right and illuminates the face of the Custodian-Moro with a candle.

MORO: You speak well. Your mind is enlivened, Yago; now you are speaking without such uproar or racket. Your own temple is a prison for you. And for me, worse yet. It is a tomb. But at least I know another time is coming.

The Custodian disappears in the darkness. The woman illuminates Santiago's face with a candle.

SANTIAGO: My soul must be in a bad, very bad, state if I can't even feel encouraged by the devastation of my enemy, nor indignant at their hope.

Santiago disappears in the darkness. The woman turns to the left, towards life again. She approaches the bench where she had fallen asleep at the beginning of the play. She illuminates her own face and blows out the candle.

END

Notes

1. *Majordomo*—This is the title given to the host or sponsor of a community festival. This honor comes with the responsibility of providing food, fireworks, and music (often a brass band), as well as other expenses including new clothes or an altar for the religious figure being celebrated.

2. "Very good, very good, how nice that you are playing your violin. Now tell us, then, where is the key? You should know where the key is, right?"

3. "What key are you talking about? Go look for the priest. He has to know where the keys are."

4. "Where could the priest be? He's not here anymore. Where could he have gone? He left. He gave you the keys."

5. "No, my father gave me this key. And you have been bothering me, for no reason, since yesterday."

6. "Not so. You're a liar like your father, you're a dirty person, like the dregs from corn-beer. Just like your father. Like everyone here. You're an Indian. Indian!"

7. "You're the liar! Dirty man! So, you want to punch it out? Well, bring it on!"

8. "Shut your mouth, you hear! You're an Indian."

9. Santiago is referring to the Battle of Cajamarca, which took place on 16 November 1532, when the Spaniards, led by Francisco Pizarro, attacked and captured the Inca ruler Atahuallpa, killing some seven thousand Indigenous inhabitants in the process.

10. Santiago refers here to the fact that the statue of the Moro is missing from the church.

11. Reference to the coat of arms of the city of Santiago de Compostela, Spain, where Saint James is said to be buried. The coat of arms is a divided azure shield, with a gold chalice on one side, and the urn of Saint James in silver on the other.

12. The play on words is lost in translation: *Caballero, ¿así te gusta cabaglar?* translates to "Horseman ("gentleman" or "knight"), is that how you like to horse ride?"

13. The play on words is lost in translation: in *Yago eres para yacer en polvo*, "Yago" is a nickname for Santiago as well as the first-person singular, present tense form of the verb *yacer*, or "to lie" (as in "to lie down," inert).

14. *Color quebrado*—"Broken colored" was a category used in colonial times to describe mixed-race peoples, whose blood was considered "impure" and the color considered "broken." The Spanish colonial caste system was intricately categorized; *color quebrado* referred to those whose racial mixture fell outside the official categories.

15. In Andean culture, twins are created through the intervention of Illapa in a mother's womb, and are thus considered special, even sacred, beings. For more on the connections of twin births and lightning, and Illapa and symbolic and practical manifestations in Andean spiritual and cultural life, see Sarah Bennison, "The Lightning's Children and My Own Child: Notes on Twin Births and Double Crowns in the *Huarochirí Mansucript*," *Indiana*, vol. 39, no. 1, 2022, pp. 201–23; and David W. Gade, "Lightning in the Folklife and Religion of the Central Andes," *Anthropos*, vol. 78, nos. 5–6, 1983, pp. 770–88.

16. Illapa was one of the most revered and powerful gods in Andean culture, along with Wiraqucha, the Creator God, and Inti, the Sun God. The idea that Santiago is the "Ruler of these High Heavens and these Caves" reinforces the Andean syncretism of the Christian saint with the Andean deity.

17. "Let's ask Mama Coca if your Patron Saint really wants to go out."

18. The rite is a "pago a la tierra," an offering to Pachamama in thanksgiving for her gifts. This rite honoring Mother Earth, a central Andean deity, points to the syncretism present in Andean religiosity.

19. In traditional *cofradías*—the Catholic lay brotherhoods in Spain and Latin America that are in charge of caring for and honoring religious images and ceremonies—men are responsible for dressing the saints. Women are supposed to clean. Bernardina is resisting her role here.

20. Juan de Santa Cruz Pachacuti Yamqui Salcamaygua was a seventeenth-century Indigenous chronicler in the Viceroyalty of Peru, known for his *Relación de las antigüedades del Reino del Perú* (*An Account of the Antiquities of Peru*; ca. 1613), a history of the Incas in Spanish, Quechua, and Aymara, with text and drawings. Its famous sketch of the Qoricancha altar presents a complex symbolic representation of the Andean worldview.

21. "What is this, my father Santiago? Why?"

22. "That's a sign from Illapa! He's walking outside! He's raining, he's shining, he's welcoming me!"

23. *Quena*—A traditional Andean flute made of reeds or wood, consisting of one long tube with six holes and one thumb hole.

24. "My father, today just now we have come to gather here. In all the towns, men and women are on their last legs. For this reason, we bring you this sweet song, which we sing from the bottom of our hearts."

25. "Great Lord Jesus Christ / Merciful Father / Have mercy / on your orphaned son."

26. "Hey, Indian, shut up! Get out of there! Corn-beer dregs face!"

27. "This is the House of Illapa. The first time he came down from the heavens to this earth, at that moment he raised a stone wall, and they turned it into this temple. Here lives the spirit of Illapa, with our father Huiracocha the Creator, with our father the Sun. And they say Santiago arrived on his white horse much later.

This radiant lightning is Illapa, and the rain is Illapa; the storm is Illapa. Or rather, Mama Coca is telling me that Illapa lives outside and wouldn't want a procession. He is furious, he's feeling hatred towards everything that they're doing. Nothing is right; these are backwards times."

28. "Oh, shut your mouth, boy. You're going to bring a punishment upon us."

29. "What punishment will I bring? More punishment will come on you, because you have failed this town of yours."

30. When martyred, St. Peter the Apostle insisted on being crucified upside down because he did not believe himself worthy to be crucified in the same way as Jesus Christ.

31. "My Father, I would go to heaven, if that is your will. My tears of longing are my open wound."

32. *Layq'a*—witch doctor or sorcerer.

33. "Now, let's drink, have some, señora."

34. The *ukukos* play a central role in the Q'oyllur Rit'i festival that takes place annually in late May or early June at the foot of the Apu Sinakara mountain in Cuzco province.

35. "No, *papito lindo* ("my dear sir"), I should go. I must go to the Q'oyllur Rit'i festival. Don't stop me." The *ukuko* is a character from the Cuzco region, which is reflected in the particularities of the Quechua he speaks.

36. "Hey, and where are you going, where are you heading with that pretty face of yours? Well, fine, ah, then I bring you this so that you can go to Q'oyllur Rit'i. Try it, please, ah . . . quite tasty, like me. It's from here, they say, nice, they say."

37. "Very well then, so tell us, where would that key be, the one we're looking for, yes?"

38. "The key you're talking about, the priest took them; I haven't seen it."

39. "Couldn't you have seen where it is? Look at the door, what's hanging there? A lock . . . then where could that key be? Help me, come on!"

40. "Come, come, I'll tell you, only you. Here is the high altar. On this side lives our mother, the Virgin Mary, in the middle, our lord Jesus Christ. And now, who do you think lives on this side? San Pedro ("Saint Peter"); he knows where the key is. Ask him, now, ha!"

41. "Hey, that's true, that San Pedro is the big guardian, and you are the little one. If this is so, where could the key be now? Ask our father (San Pedro), 'Where is the key?'"

42. "Will I ask San Pedro? Fine, fine. San Pedroooo! Bring me the key; this man wants the key. He doesn't hear; he's deaf, OK? He's already old, OK?"

43. "Get up wherever you want; just bring me the key."

44. "Shush, woman, are you listening? I bought these keys with my own money."

45. "Now we're going to open this door."

46. "So, now what? Your knight has come out. Now watch out—you're going to get it! On top of everything, you're here standing on two feet. Aren't you tired? Maybe you're wanting a mare? Are you hungry? Come, eat this green pasture, your belly sounds like an old tin can. Come eat the flowers. Your Saint needs to mount you; of course, other Gods don't need a horse. And if I let you loose, would you like to come with me to the Q'oyllur Rit'i festival?"

47. "What do I think of when seeing our Patron this way? But certainly, people said that a long time ago bad people arrived in this town, like Patron Santiago, riding a horse, shooting a rifle. In that way, they say, in the *Sunturwasi* [Quechua term for a ritual building, a place for formal events], Patron Santiago appeared on top of a gunpowder cloud, and they say he killed the gentiles, making them burn like ichu grass. Since when has there been such death? Until when? So, this year I have well seen men and women, feeling hatred in their hearts, holding machine guns, blowing dynamite; they killed the mayor, the lieutenant-mayor, the lieutenant governor, and the judge too. Because of that the priest didn't come, but only soldiers came, saying, 'Vamos a matar al enemigo' ["We're going to kill the enemy"]. And it was only at that time that no one lives in this town anymore."

48. "My father's bones are buried here, too. 'You're a thief,' they said as they killed him. We won't die here like my father."

49. "No! My father was not a thief!"

50. "Come now, Rufino, don't be sad! If our Patron makes you remember things, then let him jog your memory. Come on, ask where that Moro could be. Speak up."

51. "Why don't you ask your Patron Saint? He should know where that Moro sculpture is."

52. "Yes, our Patron hears me, but he does not respond. Instead, you make him tell you."

53. "Who could have taken him? Maybe he walked off all by himself."

54. "When has a sculpture-statue ever gone away on its own? Could it walk off?"

55. "But people say that one day the Moro just stood himself up. They say he just walked off, or that a thief stole him."

56. "If you know that, stop lying. Tell me, where did the thief take the statue? And then let's talk about thieves . . . let's talk about your father."

57. "You should know better. Aren't you the Majordomo? You either had the key taken, or you are the thief."

58. "Yes, I am the Majordomo, but I know all types of things about you and your father. Now, let's talk instead about this: I found this in a corner of your bedroom. What is it? Speak!"

59. "You are a bad omen!"

60. "Yes, your Patron has not been taken out for a procession in fifteen years. You want him to go out now? He can't, just so you know. Give me my mask, I'm asking nicely."

61. "Is this what you want? Then pick it up off the ground."

62. The *yawar mayu* ("river of blood") is a ritual battle dance performed at several Andean festivals, including the Q'oyllur Rit'i, in which participants whip one another to extract blood meant to feed Mother Earth. Inge Bolin notes, "The dance expresses many central concerns of the Quechua people, both past and present. It is a show of strength, bravery, and endurance by the men and women who today, as in Inca times, are proud of these attributes. Opposition and solidarity, complementarity and transformation, fertility and the idea of sacrifice are all part of the game" (*Rituals of Respect: The Secret of Survival in the High Peruvian Andes*, U of Texas P, 1998; 99).

About the Translator

Anne Lambright is Paul Mellon Distinguished Professor of Hispanic Studies and head of Languages, Cultures, and Applied Linguistics at Carnegie Mellon University. A citizen of the Chickasaw Nation, her scholarship centers on Indigenous studies, human rights studies, and Andean literature and cultures. Her published works include *Creating the Hybrid Intellectual: Subject, Space, and the Feminine in the Narrative of José María Arguedas* (2007) and *Andean Truths: Transitional Justice, Ethnicity, and Cultural Production in Post-Shining Path Peru* (2015).